As the men go, so goes every a~~church~~, or the culture. Strong n in the world. At no time has st needed than it is today. That is Mueller in your hands. Here is clearly presented God's blueprint for what a man should be. If every man would follow this divine design, we would see God's purpose fulfilled in their lives. Such is my hope for you as you learn and follow the timeless truths in this book.

Steven J. Lawson, President, OnePassion Ministries
Professor, The Master's Seminary
Teaching Fellow, Ligonier Ministries
Lead Preacher, Trinity Bible Church of Dallas

This book is a timely and much-needed resource. Chris Mueller has identified a number of hurdles and obstacles to a biblical understanding of manhood and addresses them with great insight and courage. In an age that denies not only the biblical, but also the scientific and common-sense realities of manhood and womanhood, we need books like this. We need men like Chris who see the threat and are willing to identify and confront it, and to do so in a way that exalts Christ and calls God's people to do the same.

Voddie Baucham, Dean of Theology, African Christian University

Sadly, there is a man crisis in God's church. The problem with the men in the local church today is not toxic masculinity or macho-manliness. The crisis is based on confusion over what it means to be a faithful man of God. Chris Mueller does an excellent job of defining biblical manhood and describing how biblical manhood functions in the home and the church for the glory of God.

Dr. Josh Buice, Pastor, Pray's Mill Baptist Church
President, G3 Ministries

In a day when boys act like girls, men act like boys, and women act like men, my friend Chris Mueller has written a timely book that takes the Word of God, and cuts through the cultural fog on gender roles. This book which borrows from Paul's writing to Titus encourages men to urgently pick up the mantle of saintly, sacrificial, sober, strategic, sensible, and strong masculinity patterned after Christ. The home, the church, and the world desperately need an infusion of biblical manhood. Therefore, I dare you to read this book.

Philip De Courcy, Senior Pastor, Kindred Community Church
Teacher, Know The Truth

We have reached a time when it is controversial to affirm that men and women are different, and that their training in Christian character would do well to not be identical. God, of course, has taken this "bold approach" in the New Testament book of Titus, and Chris Mueller has wisely followed it. In this first volume of his insightful pastoral instruction, Mueller drives home a wide variety of principles from God's Word, which all Christian men would do well to prayerfully dive into.

Dr. Mike Fabarez, President, Compass Bible Institute, Focal Point Ministries

I first met Chris Mueller 39 years ago as he was my college pastor at Grace Community Church. He taught a Sunday series called *Let the Men Be Men* which was life-changing. I had never heard such teaching before that was so biblical and applicable to me. I still remember those foundational truths today and am thrilled that these lessons have now made their way into print! With solid exposition through the book of Titus and practical application for today, this is a must read for any young man who desires to grow and mature in Christ. Thank you, Chris, for this amazing contribution to my life and for the positive impact it will have on others who read this book.

Dr. Benjamim Shin, Associate Professor, Talbot School of Theology

Finally, it's in print! I was a brand-new believer when Chris preached this series at Grace Community Church's college department. It changed my life. I wanted to be a godly man, but I had no clue how. I pray that *Let the Men be Men* gets a far and broad reading and that it becomes the new gold standard for young men like J. C. Ryle's timeless Thoughts for Young Men. Fathers, read this to your sons. Pastors, teach this to your youth. Young men, get this book today!

Bobby Scott, Pastor, Community of Faith Bible Church

The church's concept of biblical masculinity suffers from confusion and contamination. Confusion about what it means to be a real man in God's design and contamination from worldly ideas that have been integrated into its model. *Let the Men be Men* provides a reset button for this dilemma. Very simply, Mueller's volume is a biblical curriculum for what God desires and expects for biblical masculinity. This book is not only relevant to older and younger men, but is also an excellent resource for women to study. Our church will be reading this material with eagerness.

Rick Holland, Senior Pastor, Mission Road Bible Church

The current cultural crisis regarding gender and sexual identity necessitates the fearless proclamation of biblical truth regarding manhood. Chris Mueller's messages were tremendously impactful during my college years. They provided a strong foundation that was not just theory but truth put into practice. This book centralizes on the authority and sufficiency of God's Word as He is the One who designed and created what it means to be a man. This important discipleship resource is a much needed tool to raise up the next generations of godly men for God's glory.

John Kim, Senior Pastor, Lighthouse Bible Church Los Angeles

Lost in a sea of confusion, men across this country are being 'tossed here and there by waves and carried about by every wind of doctrine' (Eph 4:14). Often the false doctrine being peddled is an all-out assault on biblical masculinity. I am thankful that Chris Mueller cuts through the cultural confusion to give men a clarion call to biblical manhood. This book will be a reminder of the timeless truths God has set forth and a call for men to be humble, servant leaders that honor Christ in all things.

Dr. Scott Ardavanis, Senior Pastor, Grace Church of the Valley

LET THE
MEN
BE MEN

GOD'S DESIGN FOR
MANHOOD AND MARRIAGE

CHRIS MUELLER

FOREWORD BY JOHN MACARTHUR

Printed in the United States of America
26 25 24 23 22 / 1 2 3 4 5

ISBN: 978-1-63664-059-4

DEDICATION

To Jean Mueller,
next to Christ, my greatest love;
who partnered with me in raising two men,
Matthew John Mueller and Marc Daniel Mueller.
To them, their wives, Danielle and Breanna,
and my grandsons, Ryker, Finn and Maverick,
I dedicate this book.
My prayer is for my grandsons to one day
come to Christ, then become like Christ and live as Godly men.

ACKNOWLEDGEMENTS

I want to acknowledge my friends John and Patricia MacArthur
who more than any other, shaped my preaching, pastoring and marriage.

To the Elders of Faith Bible Church Murrieta
who are being used of God to shepherd the most amazing local church.

To the Congregation of Faith Bible Church Murrieta
for your constant love, encouragement, and walking in the truth.

To the Men of the Training Center, both current and past,
for your willingness to be trained and to pursue God's design for Men and Ministry.

To my long-standing friends and fellow pastors,
who have modeled these principles as men and love me
even though you know all my weaknesses.

To the Master's Seminary faculty and students
for being consistently biblical, and like myself,
passionately desiring to impact this world for Christ.

To Gary Kim, a collegian, who experienced the exposition of Titus 2 on men and
women, and now as a publisher, lovingly pressed me to write this book
and its partner book, *Let the Women be Women*.

To Chris Scotti and other editors, along with several members of FBC
for excellent editing and encouragement,
in the process of writing and refining *Let the Men be Men*.

TABLE OF CONTENTS

FOREWORD

BY JOHN MACARTHUR

PASTOR OF GRACE COMMUNITY CHURCH IN SUN VALLEY, CALIFORNIA

CHANCELLOR OF THE MASTER'S UNIVERSITY AND SEMINARY

PRESIDENT OF GRACE TO YOU

In 1 Corinthians 16:13, the Apostle Paul gives a clear command to "act like men." In our current times that is a difficult target for even Christian young adults to hit. The good news is that, in the book of Titus, God provides us with direct instruction on how to achieve that goal. There, the apostle Paul reveals God's clear design for how young men are to walk worthy of Jesus Christ.

I have known Chris Mueller as a friend and fellow pastor for decades. He also served alongside me at Grace Community Church for a decade before God called him to shepherd Faith Bible Church. It was during his ministry here as Grace Church's College Pastor that he originated a series from Titus called *Let the Men be Men* and *Let the Women be Women*. During this period our college students experienced incredible growth, both in numbers and spiritual maturity. I would know: most of my own children were blessed to be a part of this very ministry.

I am grateful that the content of that series, which Chris has continued to teach for several decades, is now published. In every generation, Christian men and women desperately need a biblical foundation on the roles which God designed, yet few churches give it. This book and its partner, *Let the Women be Women*, are therefore all the more valuable to meet that need.

If you are a young man, or have influence on young men, you need to absorb the truth in this book for your own sake and those you impact. If you are a young woman, you need to read this book to know what godly character qualities you should be looking for in a future husband. Certainly, young married men will benefit from the principles contained in *Let the Men be Men* since these principles are the pillars of a healthy marriage. And if you are already a mature believer, the biblical instruction in this book will refresh your pursuit of God's design for blessing and allow you to take a spiritual inventory of how you are fulfilling God's design for godly living.

While the challenges for young Christians can seem overwhelming in our current culture, God, through His Word, provides the wisdom and the power to live a life worthy of Him. I pray that this treasure of practical truth will be an encouragement to Christian young men who are fighting daily to live for our Savior's glory. And for those who are not in Christ, I hope divine instruction will awaken them to their need of the Savior to empower them, through His Spirit, to "act like men."

INTRODUCTION

LET THE MEN BE MEN: DISCOVERING THE NEED FOR MODELING AND INSTRUCTION

Be watchful, stand firm in the faith, act like men, be strong.
1 CORINTHIANS 16:13

In 1983, I was redirected from leading youth ministry to become the college pastor at Grace Community Church. The college group was in trouble and the elders trusted my leadership, so they asked me to step into a ministry that had lost its way. I was 27 years old, newly married and wondering how I could turn this ministry around.

To my surprise, the 150 collegians were hungry for sound doctrine, practical theology and pastoral leadership. I started training leaders to lead Bible studies in the future. We started dreaming about starting campus Bible studies at UCLA, USC, CAL STATE NORTHRIDGE and other nearby schools, with the goal of reaching the lost.

I started teaching on the theology of servanthood, spiritual gifts and the role every Christian has in the local church. I quickly saw collegians jump into various forms of ministry. We held garage sales to raise money for short-term missions, cleaned church properties, ministered to widows and those with disabilities. Within a couple of years, collegians were serving in almost every ministry at Grace Church.

Next, I focused on Christ's Great Commission of making disciples. I sought to define discipleship biblically as intentional relationships for the purpose of sharing the gospel and spiritual growth. Not only did I want our collegians to disciple within our group, but it was critical for the future as many would marry and one day become parents. Parenting is a form of discipleship, so getting them ready to lead the next generation was crucial.

My time with the collegians was also a lot of fun. We laughed together, cared for one another, and enjoyed great times of fellowship. Together, my wife and I watched the Lord do amazing things. The gospel was being preached and collegians were getting saved!

As I got to know these collegians, I noticed a glaring need. Women thought being a godly woman meant they must be a ministry speaker, write books and hit the Bible teaching circuit. Others were pursuing careers in business or some other field, but rarely was marriage or a family mentioned as part of their future plans.

The men had a similar misunderstanding. They all believed that the only way to become a godly man was to become a pastor or missionary. There was no mention of character, spiritual leadership, or becoming a husband and father. I realized I had to do something, but had no idea what to do.

As our campus ministries were developing, I did not have enough trained staff to minister at our seven campuses. So I looked for young married couples at Grace Church who loved Christ, held to sound doctrine and could disciple collegians. As these couples started serving in our ministry, their living examples provided a picture of what a godly (not perfect) marriage looked like and the collegians (especially those coming from broken homes) were attracted to Christ and marriage because of their example. I realized that these collegians needed to hear what God's Word says about the roles of men and women, then see God's design modeled.

I started a preaching series called, LET THE MEN BE MEN and LET THE WOMEN BE WOMEN from Titus 2:4-8. This series rocked my world and further transformed the college ministry. The ministry grew in size, but more importantly, the students (youth to young marrieds) repented and turned to Christ. It was incredible to see God do amazing things through the teaching of His Word.

Since the 1980's, God has continued to use these messages to transform lives. Gone are the days of cassette tapes, but God's truth lives on through the free downloads available on our church's website (www.faith-bible.net).

As our world moves to greater confusion and many churches fail to teach God's Word as written, the content of these books will feel more foreign to modern readers. Regardless, the goal is to honor GOD'S DESIGN for both men and women and allow the reader to wrestle with how to obey God's Word in the midst of a distorted world.

The greatest burden some readers will struggle with is the overwhelming sense that they can't live these truths. And it is true, you and I will not be able to live God's design for men or for women unless we have been born again. And as a Christian, we can't live out God's design for a man or woman, unless we are dependent upon the Holy Spirit.

Many people understand they stand condemned before a Holy God because of their sin. Therefore, they deserve to be punished forever in hell. But the merciful Father, sent His perfect Son to pay the wages of sin (which is death). Jesus Christ lived a perfect life, then offered Himself as our substitute to take the punishment we deserve for our sins. Christ rose from the dead, ascended into heaven and is the only One who can provide a way for you to be right with God. You must trust completely in the work of Christ by faith and turn from your sin in repentance to be saved. That is the doctrine of justification.

Along with being justified, if you are a genuine Christian, you will also be regenerated. A true believer is a new creation. You look the same on the outside, but you are not the same on the inside. God gives you a new heart that wants to obey His Word. And this is the only way any believer can ever obey God's Word and live out God's design for men and women.

No one can grow to be a godly man or godly woman who doesn't have Christ indwelling them and living through them in genuine salvation. Only genuine Christians have the Spirit of God empowering them to grow into God's man or God's woman in sanctification. As you begin to read this study of God's design for men, first make certain you are truly His child. I guarantee that the challenge for men, to <u>ACT LIKE MEN</u>, is impossible if you walk this journey alone. Christ dwelling in you is your only hope.

1

LET THE MEN BE MEN
CUTTING THROUGH THE CONFUSION

"And God created man in His own image, in the image of God He created him; male and female He created them."
GENESIS 1:27

"Daddy, what's the difference between boys and girls?" the little girl asked.

Her father panicked. He knew that he would have to answer that question someday, but he didn't think that day would come so soon! As his mind raced through all his preconceived answers, he struggled to respond. Wisely, he chose to pose the question back to her: "Well, what do you think is the difference between boys and girls?"

She thought for a moment, and with the air of making an incredibly astute observation, she replied, "Daddy, that's simple. Girls wear dresses and boys don't." She didn't press the issue any further, and the father sighed with relief.

STAGES OF CONFUSION

As young children grow a bit older, the differences between the sexes begin to take shape, and as a result many boys and girls hardly want to associate with each other at all. Boys think girls are "disgusting." Girls think boys are "gross." This is the season of life when boys and girls voluntarily stay apart. But as they continue to grow, a radical change occurs..

The physical differences between boys and girls become very obvious, but that doesn't deter them from wanting to spend more time together. In fact, the more different they become, the more attracted they often are to each other. They no longer voluntarily stay apart. Instead, they spend most of their time trying to answer a new question: "How can we get together?"

When I was that age, most of my conversations with guy friends involved trying to figure out how to initiate a conversation with the girls I liked. I spent a lot of time trying to figure out how to even say "hi." At one point, I became so desperate that I started calling girls and saying "hi" without telling them who I was. Many times, they started talking to me because they thought I was someone else. My plan would go along pretty smoothly until I started laughing nervously and hung up the phone.

The point is, there comes a time when both sexes start to look at each other with fascination and awe. And from that point on, the "dating game" begins. But along with this new appreciation for the opposite sex comes a great deal of confusion. At least in some circles, guys are supposed to be masculine and girls are supposed to be feminine—not only in appearance, but in their attitudes, actions, and goals. We know there are differences between the sexes. But confusion lingers as to what those differences actually are. There is no shortage of cultural influences seeking to answer the question for us. Even when we're seeking to be biblical (which is the goal of this book), we may be more influenced by our society than we think.

REASONS FOR CONFUSION

I believe there are five foundational reasons why there is such confusion about true masculinity and femininity within the church.

The first reason is our society's push toward a unisex or no-sex ideal. The unisex ideal, born out of the women's liberation movement, attempts to break down all gender distinctions to the point that one's sex—male or female—is completely irrelevant. While the women's liberation movement has had some positive impact ensuring dignity and equal rights for women, many areas of this movement depart from or directly contradict what God has laid out in Scripture.

The second reason for the confusion regarding masculinity and femininity is the LGBTQ movement. As Christians who believe the Bible is God's Word, we understand that homosexuality and transgenderism are not a part of God's design for men and women. But its pervasiveness in our culture can influence our thinking and worldview in ways we may not realize.

"...our culture can influence our thinking and worldview in ways we may not realize."

The implications of these two significant movements present more challenges. While the women's liberation movement argues that one's sexual makeup shouldn't make any difference in how one lives, the LGBTQ movement emphasizes that one's sexual makeup makes all the difference in how one lives. The world is divided not into male and female, but gay, straight, bisexual, transgender, non-binary, and a growing list of other labels. While these two movements were intended to be liberating, they have resulted in a variety of complications, especially for young men and women. Every time someone fails to measure up to the vague understanding of masculine and feminine ideals it can cause confusion. A man may wonder if he might be homosexual, or perhaps a woman trapped in a man's body. Or he may buy into a popular deception—that there are dozens of genders.

The third reason for the confusion about gender is the breakdown of marriage. You may have experienced your parents' divorce, or may have grown up in a single-parent home. You may not have up-close experience seeing how men and women can live together in a biblical way. You may not have grown up with an admirable, godly father. And when we lack real-life examples, there is a greater tendency to develop our views of manhood and womanhood based on an assortment of television shows, movies, and other media. We do our best to live out our God-given gender, but without a biblical model, we are not really sure how to act, which compounds our anxiety and confusion.

The fourth reason is the distortion of gender roles paraded in social media, entertainment, news outlets, and secular education. In contrast to God's view, young men and women are continually bombarded with anti-biblical views on the roles of men and women. We even find these immoral ideologies embedded into kindergarten through university class curriculum.

The fifth reason for confusion is that there is a significant lack of accurate and gutsy teaching of biblical truth in this area. Even in churches and institutions professing to have sound doctrine, there is an absence of true biblical instruction on what men and women are to be, based on the actual text of Scripture. This lack of boldness in unapologetically proclaiming and living out the truths of God's Word is a massive problem.

EXAMPLES OF CONFUSION

Where does all of this leave us? For many individuals, these conflicting messages result in a perpetual state of internal conflict.

For example, you may have a conflict concerning your identity. You begin to ask questions like these: *Who am I really? What kind of person am I supposed to be? How am I supposed to act in certain situations?*

For men, in particular, we might ask these questions: *Should I cry or should I mask my emotion? What happens when we're in a group and another guy cries? How should the rest of us respond to that?* If we are being honest, we know it is uncomfortable to not truly understand who we are supposed to be. Should we act tough and unaffected, or be gentle and kind? Do we work at being strong and muscular, or is it fine if we lack physical strength? Do we become a flirtatious ladies' man, or work at being God's man? And whatever we choose, what difference does it make?

It isn't merely the young men who struggle with issues of identity and life choices, of course. The questions women wrestle with may include: *Should I pursue a career or wait to be married? Should I study more and pursue advanced degrees or focus on becoming a wife and mother? Do I try to let the guy lead, or should I tell him when he's acting like a fool?* These are all difficult questions the next book in this series, *Let The Women Be Women*, will deal with.

The conflict is also seen in our relationships with the opposite sex. In fact, if we don't really know who we're supposed to be as individuals, we can't possibly know how to interact properly with the opposite sex.

"... if we don't really know who we're supposed to be as individuals, we can't possibly know how to interact properly with the opposite sex."

If you have experienced that confusion in your own life, please know that you are not alone. I can relate. In fact, when I was in college, I was really confused too. I didn't understand who I was supposed to be. And that became clear through the friendships and dating relationships I had with girls at the time.

The first girl I ever seriously dated as a Christian and built a strong friendship with had just become a new creation in Christ. When we decided it was better to remain friends than seek to move our relationship forward, she began to take off spiritually. I realized that I had been holding her back because I wasn't comfortable with who I was, and as a result, I wasn't letting her be all that God intended her to be. I had hindered her spiritual growth.

The second girl I built a relationship with was godly and extremely knowledgeable about Scripture. In fact, she went on to become a missionary. She really was the spiritual leader in our relationship. After the relationship ended, I was frustrated because I realized that I should have been the spiritual leader. I really needed to know God's Word better, make decisions based on Scripture, and gently lead in our relationship. I should have encouraged her and built her up spiritually instead of her building me up spiritually.

So I took a long break from dating because I needed to figure out who and what God wanted me to be.

After about a year and a half, I began to date another girl. She was a fireball who wanted to change the world. She was brilliant and went on to earn a PhD. She was attractive, athletic, an effective minister, strong, independent, dogmatic, and competitive. She beat me all the time at racquetball. And I still didn't understand male headship, spiritual leadership, and what God expected of me. I still didn't really know what I was looking for in a potential spouse, and in God's providence, she and I never seemed to have enough time together to develop our friendship.

By the time I met my future wife Jean, all I wanted was to do things God's way by following the teaching of Scripture. She was godly, knew God's Word, was driven to serve Christ, desired to be a pastor's wife, and was very beautiful. After being friends for a while, our trust and respect for one another grew. It became obvious I needed to take the next step, so I sought counsel from the godliest man I knew, my mentor John MacArthur, and asked if he thought I should date Jean. He rolled back in his chair, laughed out loud, and said, "What took you so long?" He performed our marriage ceremony about nine months later.

Over the years, my view of what I am supposed to be as a man before God has come into sharper focus. And my understanding of biblical womanhood has become clearer as well. If I had known these things back in my college days, not only would I have been more content, but I also would have avoided hurting a lot of other people, sadly even the women I cared about.

THE WAY OUT OF CONFUSION

Take a few moments right now to stop and ask yourself a few questions.

The first is this: What do you really want to be? Not what you want to do, but who do you really want to be? And be specific.

Once you answer, ask yourself a second question: Who does God want you to be?

The final question is this: Are those two answers the same? If they're not, are you willing to change and become who God wants you to be? Can you be humble enough to lay down your life before God and commit to learning and living according to Scripture?

Only through God's Word and by the power of His Holy Spirit can men and women know who God wants them to be. Only if we approach the Word of God with an attitude of total humility, submission, and obedience can we swim against the tide of our society and live out God's design for us. A section of Scripture where God speaks most clearly and specifically about His will for young men and young women is in the book of Titus. But before jumping into particular verses, we need to understand the book of Titus as a whole.

"A section of Scripture where God speaks most clearly and specifically about His will for young men and young women is in the book of Titus."

Paul's reason for writing his letter to Titus is found in Titus 1:16: "They profess to know God, but by their works they deny Him, being detestable and disobedient and unfit for any good work." The main problem with the church on the island of Crete was false teachers who spoke some truth but did not live it out. Throughout this letter, we see a recurring theme that the true Christian—and the true Christian teacher—will practice good works (1:16; 2:7, 14; 3:1, 8, 14).

Paul's emphasis on genuine Christians producing good fruit is another way of saying that faith without works is dead (James 2:17). Paul's master solution to the problem of teachers who don't live out the truth is found in Titus 1:5: "For this reason I left you in Crete, that you would set in order what remains and appoint elders in every city as I directed you." The men who lead the church must not only teach the truth but live the truth. And if they don't, they are rebellious men, empty talkers, and deceivers (1:10).

Merely knowing sound doctrine isn't enough—it must be manifested in our lives. If we take in biblical teaching but don't respond in obedience, there's a problem.

At the start of Chapter 2, Paul exhorts Titus to speak the things which are fitting for sound doctrine. And at the end of chapter 2, Paul says, "These things speak and exhort and reprove with all authority. Let no one disregard you" (v. 15). It seems clear that Paul anticipated that people would reject his words in chapter 2—words that are addressed to older men, older women, young men, and young women about what God expects of them and His particular design for their lives. Here's what Paul wrote that was so controversial:

> *Older men are to be temperate, dignified, sensible, sound in faith, in love, in perseverance. Older women likewise are to be reverent in their behavior, not malicious gossips nor enslaved to much wine, teaching what is good, so that they may instruct the young women in sensibility: to love their husbands, to love their children, to be sensible, pure, workers at home, kind, being subject to their own husbands, so that the word of God will not be slandered. Likewise urge the younger men to be sensible; in all things show yourself to be a model of good works, with purity in doctrine, dignified, sound in word which is irreproachable, so that the opponent will be put to shame, having nothing bad to say about us (vv. 2–8).*

If you were to rate yourself on the characteristics laid out for men in that passage, how would you do? If the number one represented non-existent and the number ten was perfect, which number would represent you? How would you measure up? What number would you give yourself between one and ten?

For all of us, the focus is to learn and live out the Word of God. Does that describe you? Do you daily meditate on His Word? Could you prove the deity of Christ to an unbeliever from Scripture? Could you answer someone's questions about perceived discrepancies in the Bible? Could you teach a child about the Trinity? Could you help your friends with what the Bible says about divorce? Are you ready? Do you really know the Word?

Men, if you want to grow, you will not only need to learn what God's Word says but also be a doer of the Word. You will have to learn from older godly men. So let me ask you another question: Do you model your life after someone who is older and more mature in his Christian life than you are? I'm not talking about discipleship, though that is essential. I'm simply talking about modeling. Who do you watch? Does he provide the right example? And are you ready to imitate his lifestyle?

> ## "Do you model your life after someone who is older and more mature in his Christian life than you are?"

GOOD NEWS!

If you're feeling overwhelmed already at the beginning of this book, I have good news for you. The book of Titus is not a list of rules to obey or commands to follow in your own strength. It's not merely about "being a better man." Rather, this Epistle called Titus is grounded in the person and work of Jesus Christ and the power of the Holy Spirit.

In Chapter 2 of Titus we also read,

> *For the grace of God has appeared, bringing salvation to all men, instructing us that, denying ungodliness and worldly desires, we should live sensibly, righteously and godly in the present age, looking for the blessed hope and the appearing of the glory of our great God and Savior, Jesus Christ, who*

gave Himself for us that He might redeem us from all lawlessness, and purify for Himself a people for His own possession, zealous for good works (vv. 11–14).

And likewise, in Titus 3:

For we ourselves also once were foolish, disobedient, deceived, enslaved to various lusts and pleasures, spending our life in malice and envy, despicable, hating one another. But when the kindness and affection of God our Savior appeared, He saved us, not by works which we did in righteousness, but according to His mercy, through the washing of regeneration and renewing by the Holy Spirit, whom He poured out upon us richly through Jesus Christ our Savior, so that having been justified by His grace, we would become heirs according to the hope of eternal life (vv. 3–7).

These passages are packed with the grace, mercy, and love of God for His people. The Father is the architect of our salvation. The Son secures our salvation through His perfectly righteous life and substitutionary death on our behalf. The Holy Spirit empowers us to turn from sin and emulate our righteous Savior. And our ultimate hope is the return of Christ and the new heavens and new earth. This is the hope of the born again believer.

As we embark on this journey of learning what God says about manhood, we can only do so once we have experienced the stunning grace of God and the beauty of the person of Jesus Christ. And because we love the One who modeled perfect manhood during His thirty-plus years on earth, we want to learn to become more like Him so that He receives honor and praise through our lives. For any young man, there is no greater life-long journey than to diligently pursue God's design for men.

FOR PERSONAL REFLECTION & GROUP DISCUSSION:

1. Describe the kind of man that you want to be in the future.

2. Describe the kind of man you think God wants you to be.

3. How are your answers to the first two questions similar, and how are they different? Regarding the similarities, how do you think you can become that kind of man? Regarding the differences, what goals do you need to change or re-prioritize?

4. What questions do you have about men's or women's roles?

5. Are you one who needs to come to Christ in salvation, or one who needs to become like Christ in sanctification? How do you know which one you are?

2

LET THE MEN BE LEADERS
LOVING HEADSHIP UNDER CHRIST

"So husbands ought also to love their own wives as their own bodies. He who loves his own wife loves himself."
EPHESIANS 5:28

When I was a young boy, I remember loving local carnivals. I liked the crowds, the grandstand show, the exhibits—but most of all, I enjoyed the rides and sideshows. At one carnival, the biggest sideshow attraction was a two-headed monster. I gathered up my courage and bought my ticket. As I went in, I was horrified and fascinated to see a cow with a second head growing out of its neck at an angle. It was grotesque!

A two-headed anything is a freak of nature—and that applies to marriage as well. As we will see, just like a two-headed cow, a two-headed marriage is not the norm. According to God's timeless and perfect design, men and women were created to function in unique and different roles. God as the Creator makes all things beautiful and His design for marriage is that the husband be the head.

Why is male headship considered such an offense today? Why is it that so many couples remove the word "obey" from their wedding vows? Why are many marriages today more like a two-headed monster than a beautiful union of two becoming one?

The answer is that in this increasingly postmodern age, both men and women are not fulfilling their God-given roles. And the greatest problem is that men do not understand what it means to function as the head in marriage or their home, nor do they understand God's design for the sexes.

So before we study the design, qualities, and function of the godly man in Titus 2, it is necessary to take a focused look at the overall biblical teaching about male headship.

HEADSHIP DESIGNED AND DISTORTED

What is headship? In order to practically live out this concept, we have to look at what the Bible says, then explore the theological implications. Don't skip this part, because the truth in it will be liberating to you as a young man.

"To understand why so many people have a problem with male headship and why God's design for male and female is in such a state of confusion, you have to go all the way back to His original blueprint in Genesis 2 and 3."

In 1 Corinthians 11:3 when Paul says, "But I want you to understand that Christ is the head of every man, and the man is the head of a woman, and God is the head of Christ," what does he mean? The Greek word Paul uses here for "head" (kephale) is defined as "authority" or "direction." Two important questions remain. What kind of authority is envisioned by male headship? And what kind of direction is a Christian man expected to give to his wife?

CREATION AND FALL

To understand why so many people have a problem with male headship and why God's design for male and female is in such a state of confusion, you have to go all the way back to His original blueprint in Genesis 2 and 3.

In Genesis 2:18, God says of the man He had created, "It is not good for the man to be alone; I will make him a helper suitable for him." Next, Genesis 2:19 describes the creation of the animal world and the naming of all the animals by Adam. Genesis 2:20 points out, "And the man gave names to all the cattle and to the birds of the sky and to every beast of the field; but for Adam there was not found a helper suitable for him." Finally, in Genesis 2:21–22, we see that God provided Adam with a helper—the woman—to aid Adam as he ruled over God's creation.

From the very beginning, God designed someone to be in charge, and He designed someone to help. God made someone to be in authority and someone to submit to that authority. God created someone to be the provider, and someone for whom to provide. From the very beginning, the man had the place of headship (authority or leadership) and the woman is the one for whom that headship is provided. This is God's perfect design.

Adam is first introduced to his wife in Genesis 2:23, and he exclaims, "This one finally is bone of my bones, and flesh of my flesh; This one shall be called Woman, Because this one was taken out of Man." God then adds this postscript through Moses in Genesis 2:24: "Therefore a man shall leave his father and his mother, and cleave to his wife; and they shall become one flesh."

This first union of man and woman as husband and wife was a marvelous, perfect relationship. Adam viewed Eve in every sense as one with him. This was God's design. He was the leader, and she was to follow his lead, but in such perfect balance that the roles were always mutually beneficial within their oneness. The woman's submissiveness and the man's headship were both willing and beautiful. There was no animosity, no struggle, and no conflict in this glorious union—only a healthy partnership of supernatural oneness, which reflects the nature of the Triune God Himself: each Divine Person is unique, but there is one God (1 Corinthians 11:3).

But then something monumental occurred in Genesis 3. The serpent bypassed the headship of the man and went to the one who was by nature the follower. He enticed the woman to do the one thing God had told them not to do—eat of the fruit of the tree of the knowledge of good and evil. She took the fruit, ate it, gave it to her husband, and he ate it. In that series of events, the roles were officially reversed. Adam failed in his leadership, the woman usurped his authority, and the man became the follower. At that moment of temptation, God's design for marriage was twisted. What has resulted from the Fall has been the defilement of marriage and the corruption of God's design for men and women.

Since that first reversal of the roles, marriages have faced great difficulty. We have been cursed, which means the most basic elements of human life have been affected. In childbearing, for example, hopeful anticipation is temporarily overshadowed by the physical pain of childbirth.

The marriage relationship itself will have major problems. The man will seek to rule over the woman while the woman will seek to rule over the man. Provision for each household will be affected in that the man will have to labor and sweat in order to provide for his family. Life itself will be altered. God said to Adam concerning his partaking of the fruit of the forbidden tree, "for in the day that you eat from it you will surely die" (Genesis 2:17). Spiritual and physical death are directly the result of the sin that was committed in the Garden. God's Word teaches us that, when Adam sinned, death and sin "spread to all men" (Romans 5:12).

The human race itself has been cursed. But even in that curse, we see God's mercy. We did not immediately die physically, and the hardship of the curse itself drives men and women back to a place of dependence upon God.

In addition to the sin and curse that results from the Fall, Satan attacks the home relentlessly. With an ever-declining society (Romans 1:18–32), good is being called evil, and evil is called good (Isaiah 5:20). Marriage is now often mocked as outdated, unnecessary and evil. Some even consider God's design for a husband and wife abusive. All forms of media continually make fun of "the traditional family," to the point that believers are embarrassed to uphold God's design for marriage. Rarely will believers boldly proclaim the headship of a husband and the submission of a wife. It is no wonder that the nature and practice of marriage is increasingly in a state of chaos.

Because of the Fall recorded in Genesis 3, today we have radical women's liberation movements. Because of the Fall recorded in Genesis 3, we have the existence of male chauvinism. Because of the Fall, there is pornography, homosexuality, and transgender confusion. All of these and more are manifestations of sin, fallenness, depravity, and the curse.

EFFECTS OF THE FALL ON MEN

Why do men abuse women, fail to communicate with their wives, suppress their wives or other women, or turn women into sex objects? This all happens because of the presence and power of sin that began with the Fall.

That first sin not only separated us from our Creator and cast us out of heaven, but also had drastic effects upon the role of a man and his relationship to his wife. As a result of the Fall, men in particular have been prone to follow various ungodly and sinful models of behavior.

"As a result of the Fall, men in particular have been prone to follow various ungodly and sinful models of behavior."

The default practice for some men (even Christian husbands) is to become **dictators**. In some Christian homes, men act more like frustrated drill sergeants who run around with a biblical club saying, "I am the leader of this home!" Men like this shout out orders and demand instant obedience to every whim, meeting all opposition with verbal or physical force. Too many men run their homes as Pharaoh would, rather than modeling Christlike behavior. They want submission that is brainless, senseless and absolutely obedient, rather than voluntary, from a heart of respect. But the Christian husband is to be the head of his home (and specifically, his wife) as Christ is the head of the church (Ephesians 5:23). A Christian husband should not be the man who seeks to cram his rules down anyone's throat. Instead, he draws people to himself by the way he loves them and leads them using the Bible, empowered by the Spirit of God, manifesting the fruit of the Spirit in the process.

For other men, their base desire is to be **revered**. The flaw with this type of perspective, however, is that being the head does not guarantee that a wife and a family will automatically respect the head of the household from their hearts. Further, even if a wife wants to recognize her husband's God-given position as head, it does not mean she will respect her husband's behavior and decisions when they are sinful or foolish. Trust and respect are two absolutely essential requirements in marriage, but they are earned by a man's character, lifestyle, and spiritual maturity, not by his gender or position as the head of the home.

Some men feel they need to be the **solo decision-maker**. But the Word of God does not teach that a husband makes all the decisions. Rather, he is responsible for all the decisions that are made (Ephesians 5:22–24). Many wives, including my own wife, are gifted and experts in many areas. How foolish it would be for us as husbands to ignore the insights that the Spirit of God has given to our wives! While headship does mean authority and direction, it does not mean the husband is the sole decision-maker in the home. Marriage means oneness, and oneness implies open communication and marital cooperation. It is the pursuit of oneness in marriage that leads to like-mindedness and harmony.

Some men view themselves as the **infallible authority** in their homes. Yes, God's design is for the husband to have the role of headship. He will have to give an account to God of his stewardship as head of his home, but he will not always be right. God will never hold the wife responsible for the foolish decisions made by her husband—He will hold her responsible for how she responds to her husband's leadership. Wives need to allow their husbands grace to make mistakes.

No husband is perfect. When a husband makes a mistake, his wife cannot allow it to shake her. She must remember that God is sovereign over all, that He is all-wise, and that Christ loves her more than her husband does. Therefore, she can trust God even when her husband fails to lead biblically. When there is a disagreement between a husband and wife about a decision, it is important to have a full discussion of the matter in which all points of view are valued and considered. It is then the responsibility of the man to make that decision. Remember, honoring God and seeking humility throughout the decision making process is always the goal.

Finally, there are men who consider themselves to be the **superior species**. To say that a woman is inferior because she submits herself willingly to her husband is to say, in effect, that Jesus Christ is inferior because He submitted Himself to the will of the Father after the incarnation. That would be heresy, of course, because Jesus Christ is no less God than God the Father is—He was merely fulfilling a different role. Christ is equal, ontologically, with God the Father. Similarly, men and women are totally equal with one another from an ontological and spiritual standpoint. In fact, in Galatians 3:28 Paul says, "There is no male and female, for you are all one in Christ Jesus." As people made in the image of God, husbands and wives are equal; as marriage partners, however, there is a functional difference between the two. That difference is rooted in responsibilities that were designed by God.

So if a man of God is not supposed to be a dictator, the revered one, the solo decision-maker, the infallible authority, or the superior species, who is he to be? How is he to behave?

"As people made in the image of God, husbands and wives are equal; as marriage partners, however, there is a functional difference between the two. That difference is rooted in responsibilities that were designed by God."

Our in-depth study of Titus 2 (and other related passages) in the coming chapters will give us a large part of the answer. The godly man who is a true spiritual leader in his home is to be mentally sensible (how he thinks), an example of good works (how he serves), theologically pure (what he believes and how he lives out those beliefs), socially dignified (how he earns respect), and verbally sound in speech (what he communicates and teaches).

But before we unpack each of these traits of a godly man in the coming chapters, some further discussion of male headship from Ephesians 5:22–33 will be helpful. We've learned so far about what men should not do in their role as head; this important section of Scripture reveals what we should do, and whom we should seek to imitate.

HEADSHIP REDEEMED AND RESTORED

Before a husband's role in his marriage can be evaluated in accordance with God's Word in Ephesians 5:22–33, the husband must first be assured that he is "in Christ." You can't study Ephesians 5 without considering what Paul has already taught in chapters 1–4. These earlier chapters teach that salvation causes a dramatic change in our lives. Ephesians 1–3 describes a person who was spiritually dead and then miraculously made alive. That kind of salvation goes beyond being "religious" or merely professing to be a Christian. Instead, it means the husband must be a born-again believer who has Christ living in him and empowering him through the Holy Spirit to live as a Christian by obeying the written Word of God.

THE PREREQUISITES OF BIBLICAL HEADSHIP

The godly husband described in Ephesians 5 has been saved by grace alone, through faith alone, in Christ alone (Ephesians 1–3). He was dead but was made alive solely by the Person and work of Christ (Ephesians 2:4–5). And now this man has an entirely new life which is marked by good works done for God's glory (Ephesians 2:10).

Ephesians 4 teaches that the godly husband is a man who seeks to live (or "walk") worthy of what Christ has done for him. He is also fully interconnected with the local church. Being equipped by the Word of God that is preached, he is doing his part in ministry so that the entire church body grows to be more like Christ (Ephesians 4:11–16).

This genuine believer is also one who is continually filled with the Holy Spirit in obedience to the Word of God, (Ephesians 5:18). To be filled with the Spirit is to live life in dependence upon the Word of God while exercising your will to walk in obedience. The Christian life is not merely a moral code of conduct—do this, do that. It is not *do, do, do*; it is D.O.—Dependent Obedience.

Being filled with the Spirit is essential to living for Christ. If you are not in the Spirit, then you are in the flesh. If you are not living in God's strength, then you are living in your own strength.

Being filled with the Spirit means you are saturated in God's Word, walking in obedience to the Scriptures, dependent upon the Spirit of God to work through you, confessing all known sin, serving in the body of Christ and sharing the gospel to the lost.

In light of the reality of the divine curse on mankind, the inevitability of Satan's attacks on God's children, and the tragedy

"...only those who are Spirit-indwelt, born-again believers will ever have the resources needed to live according to God's divine will as revealed in His Word."

of the modern cultural confusion over male and female roles, only those who are Spirit-indwelt, born-again believers will ever have the resources needed to live according to God's divine will as revealed in His Word. Only those filled with the Spirit will ever be able to grow to become truly godly young men. Only those clinging moment-by-moment to the Spirit of Truth and living by the Word of Truth can ever hope to exhibit the qualities that we will learn about from Titus 2, or even those described here in Ephesians 5.

THE PRACTICE OF BIBLICAL HEADSHIP

What are the marks of the man who pursues the biblical headship described in Ephesians 5:22–33? To honor Christ and live for the glory of God." This passage contains only two commands, and they are both directed at husbands to love their wives. Biblical headship is loving headship. Verse 25 summarizes the role of the husband by saying, "Husbands, love your wives, just as Christ also loved the church and gave Himself up for her". The rest of the passage describes the perfect love of Christ that husbands are to emulate.

Sacrificial love. The word Paul uses here for "love" is *agapao*, which is the strongest, most intimate term for love. Yes, there is to be authority in a marriage. There is to be one who is the head, and there is to be one who follows. But verse 25 does not say "Husbands, rule your wives" or "Husbands, subjugate your wives" or "Husbands, command your wives." Rather, the text says this: "Husbands, love your wives." For a man to exercise biblical headship and to accept the responsibility of leadership before God, the husband must emphatically love his wife—and love her sacrificially. Biblical agape love has been defined in many ways, but one of my favorites is "a Spirit-created desire of the heart for the spiritual good of others, which produces self-sacrificial actions on their behalf." Romans 5:5 and Galatians 5:22 confirm that biblical love is produced by the Spirit, stems from the heart, and ultimately results in seeking the best for another, most often through sacrificial actions. The authority given to a husband to lead his wife is not based upon ruling, commanding, or subjugating her. Rather, it is based on an internal Spirit-created love that leads a man to sacrifice himself for his wife. His responsibility is to model Christ and follow God's Word. Such sacrificial love has multiple dimensions.

First, sacrificial love has no limits. There is a story told about a husband who once came to a famous preacher and said, "Sir, I think I'm guilty of loving my wife too much." To which the preacher replied, "Have you died for her?" The startled man said, "No!" and the preacher said, "Then you don't love her enough." You will never experience the love necessary to lead your wife—or wife-to-be—unless you are called upon to die for her, or at least come to the place where you are willing to die for her.

Second, sacrificial love provides. A godly man sacrificially loves his wife by working to support her. Biblically, the burden of caring financially for the family falls upon the man. A husband must be a provider so that:

    a. A mother of young children can keep house
       (1 Timothy 5:14)
    b. A wife can be a worker at home (Titus 2:5)
    c. A wife and mother can watch over the ways of her
       household (Proverbs 31:27)

Men are called to fulfill their roles as providers so that their spouses can fulfill their roles—as wives and mothers—in accordance with Titus 2:4–5. But husbands also provide for their households because the Bible gives direction and warning to those men who fail to care for their families. For instance, 1 Timothy 5:8 says, "But if anyone does not provide for his own, and especially for those of his household, he has denied the faith and is worse than an unbeliever." 2 Thessalonians 3:10 says, "If anyone is not willing to work, neither let him eat."

No one becomes a godly man in a day, so the challenge to

younger men is to make educational and employment decisions now—as single men, which will ultimately enable them to provide for their future wife and children.

Finally, sacrificial love repents first. When an argument flares up in a marriage, the husband should be the first one to humble himself and ask forgiveness for whatever was wrong in his behavior. The husband needs to die to self. While it may be that the wife's guilt is as great or greater, it ultimately does not matter. The man's call is to love his wife as Christ loved the church. Jesus humbled Himself and bore the guilt of our sin "while we were yet sinners" (Romans 5:8). He did not wait until we deserved His sacrifice—that would have never happened—but took the initiative to do what was necessary in order to restore our relationship with Himself. He died for His enemies (Romans 5:10). Christ's sacrifice was one-sided. When accused, He was silent. He was innocent yet made no defense.

Relating this to the marriage relationship, a godly husband does not allow his wife's sin to continue to hamper their marital oneness, and above all, does not keep a mental list of offenses. He simply goes the way of the cross, initiating the act of love by denying himself and giving up his own rights. He humbles himself before his wife to restore the relationship, because this is God's call to him as a husband. This is spiritual leadership. This is headship. Yes, there will be times when gentle confrontation of sin must occur, but when sin has caused a wall between them,

> **"The gateway to all spiritual life and blessing is repentance. As the spiritual head of the family, the husband and father must be the first to repent."**

it is the husband's responsibility to humbly tear that wall down and start the process of reconciliation. The gateway to all spiritual life and blessing is repentance. As the spiritual head of the family, the husband and father must be the first to repent. This is what it means to be a servant-leader.

Responsible love (or authoritative love). Ephesians 5:22–24 says, "Wives, be subject to your own husbands, as to the Lord. For the husband is the head of the wife, as Christ also is the head of the church, He Himself being the Savior of the body. But as the church is subject to Christ, so also the wives ought to be to their husbands in everything." A true man of God does not think of headship as his right, but as his responsibility. Headship is not so much about power as it is about duty. Just as an elder will give an account to Christ for the flock he shepherds (Hebrews 13:17), the husband will one day have to answer to Christ for the way he shepherds his wife and his children. Just as Christ is the Savior of the body, the husband is the protector of his wife and family. He is to watch over the spiritual, mental, emotional, financial, social, and physical health of his family. He must be on duty, on guard, watchful, and most of all, responsible. Since this is the case, when there is a disagreement and all has been discussed fully, then it is the husband who ultimately must decide.

Now, there is a danger that comes with this authority, which is why Colossians 3:18–19 says, "Wives, be subject to your husbands, as is fitting in the Lord. Husbands, love your wives and do not be embittered against them." Even though the husband has this headship responsibility, the man must not be harsh or bitter toward his wife. The husband is not to speak to his bride with impatience or thoughtlessness. He is to avoid fault-finding and perpetual irritation. The husband is not permitted to avoid his wife or stop choosing to love her, even if she becomes embittered against him. The godly husband honors his wife, viewing her as far more precious than expensive jewels and praising her to others, as well as personally esteeming her in his heart. He recognizes her talents, appreciates her efforts, considers her feelings, and trusts her fully. As a result, his leadership is not a yoke upon her but a joy to rest in.

Many single believers and new husbands wrongly embrace "responsible love" with a heavy hand. Most need to correct their perception of male leadership in marriage. In forty years of marriage, (that's 14,600 days, or 262,800 waking hours) I may have asked my wife to submit to my decision only twice. A husband asking his wife to submit to his decision should be extremely rare.

When a Christian couple pursues God's Word by: (1) walking in God's Spirit; (2) seeking to live out their biblically designed roles; (3) trusting and respecting each other; and (4) desiring to be one in marriage; there will rarely be a need to impose submission.

I want to know what my wife thinks about everything. She is a godly woman and very wise. Jean and I seek to work together as one in our marriage and in every aspect of life. Healthy biblical marriages function far more as a partnership than an authority structure.

Purifying love. Ephesians 5:25–27 says that Jesus gave Himself for the church "So that He might sanctify her, having cleansed her by the washing of water with the word, that He might present to Himself the church in all her glory, having no spot or wrinkle or any such thing, but that she would be holy and blameless." When we express agape love for someone, that person's purity is our supreme concern. True love never wants to defile the person who is loved. Christ loves His church, so He wants to purify His people. These verses teach us that marriage involves a purification. If a man genuinely loves his wife, he seeks to keep her feet clean from the dirt of the world, doing everything in his power to maintain her holiness, virtue, and purity. He would never join her in sin or do anything that would lead her to sin or provoke her to sin.

A husband's purifying love will even refuse to expose his wife to evil. This means being extremely careful about where he takes her, what he shows her, what he does with her, and what he allows

"Believers have been made free, but it is a freedom to obey and please Christ, not a freedom to embrace compromise, sin, or evil."

to be accepted into their home. Romans 16:19 says, "I want you to be wise in what is good and innocent in what is evil." Believers have been made free, but it is a freedom to obey and please Christ, not a freedom to embrace compromise, sin, or evil. A godly young man is more focused on living to please Christ than living to please himself; his focus is living by principle, not preferences. A godly man has a love which is pure. This must especially be true in your exposure to media. Most forms of media are not evil in themselves, but so much of the entertainment available on these platforms is impure.

In addition, the godly husband will wash his wife with the Word. Just as Christ sanctifies and cleanses the church with the Word of God (Ephesians 5:26), the true man of God will seek to instruct his wife with the Word. 1 Corinthians 14:34–35 states, "The women are to keep silent in the churches, for they are not permitted to speak, but are to subject themselves, just as the Law also says. But if they desire to learn anything, let them ask their own husbands at home, for it is disgraceful for a woman to speak in church."

Real men long for the Word of God to permeate their marriage. Godly men let the Word of God lead their homes; they lead by following the Word of God; they lead by initiating a dependence upon the Word. They typically do not tell their wives, "Do as I say." Rather, they say, "Let's do as Christ says." They make the Word of God a continual presence and source of wisdom in their home so that their wife and children are repeatedly washed in it. Godly marriages make the Scripture the filter as to what is said, and the lens through which everything is viewed.

A godly husband seeks to meet the spiritual needs of his wife. In Ephesians 5:27, Paul says the Lord wants to "present to Himself the church in all her glory, having no spot or wrinkle or any such thing, but that she would be holy and blameless." Christ is completing the process of sanctification for His bride. In a similar

> ## "...a godly husband longs for his wife to be complete in Christ—he seeks to fulfill his wife's needs so that she will grow in sanctification as a believer."

manner, a godly husband longs for his wife to be complete in Christ—he seeks to fulfill his wife's needs so that she will grow in sanctification as a believer. This is how a man must care for his wife. He should never do anything that would cause her to look to someone else for fulfillment.

Ideally, a wife should not have to depend on her father or mother or others for answers—a godly husband should be the primary resource for his wife and children. It is the husband's responsibility to meet her needs, especially as it relates to encouraging her growth in Christ. 1 Thessalonians 4:3–5 says, "For this is the will of God, your sanctification: that you abstain from sexual immorality; that each of you know how to possess his own vessel in sanctification and honor, not in lustful passion, like the Gentiles who do not know God." The godly man's central aim is not what he can get from his wife, but instead how he can honor her, keep her pure, and help her to mature in Christ.

His goal is to protect his wife from evil in the world, to set her apart uniquely for Christ, and be her number-one encourager in her pursuit of sanctification.

Sensitive and caring love. Ephesians 5:28 says, "So husbands ought also to love their own wives as their own bodies. He who loves his own wife loves himself". People generally spend a lot of time on their own bodies—exercising, checking the mirror, eating the right food, wearing nice clothes, and so on. They take care of themselves and keep their body functioning well, because the Christian's body is the temple of the Holy Spirit.

So Paul says that husbands "ought also to love their wives as their own bodies." This kind of love involves a husband sacrificing himself for his wife's needs in the same way that he sacrifices time, money, and attention to make sure he is washed, exercised, fed, and clothed. Husbands are to care for wives as they themselves care for their own needs. They no longer make solo decisions, but always consider the thoughts and opinions of their wives. They no longer do as they please, but remember they are one with their bride. It is no longer I and me, but us and we. Husbands are God's agents to care for their wives in a nourishing and cherishing way. Ephesians 5:29 adds this thought: "For no one ever hated his own flesh, but nourishes and cherishes it, just as Christ also does the church."

The Bible affirms that the Lord does care for His church. But does He supply the church with everything that the church wants? No. But does Christ provide the church with all she needs? Absolutely. In a similar way, God is telling husbands to supply everything their wives need. We nourish and cherish them as if they were literally a part of our physical body.

The Greek word for "nourish" was primarily used in reference to nurturing or bringing up children. It basically means "to mature, to feed." We men are called to nurture our wives, to help them grow to spiritual maturity. The word "cherish" means "to soften or warm with body heat," and is used to describe a mother bird as she sits on her nest. Husbands are to provide a warm, safe environment for their wife and children. Husbands are to provide security, a place of comfort, and a home environment that kindles others toward spiritual growth.

How does a man live out this kind of sensitive and caring love? 1 Peter 3:7 provides great insight: "You husbands in the same way, live with your wives in an understanding way, as with a weaker vessel, since she is a woman; and show her honor as a fellow heir of the grace of life, so that your prayers will not be hindered." The man committed to demonstrating this type of love will show great consideration. He will live with her "in an understanding way," which means to treat her the way Jesus Christ would. He will feel what she feels, talk when she needs it, and listen even when he does not think he has enough time. Godly men move beyond trying to fix their wives' problems to understanding, listening, and sacrificing to meet their spouse's needs.

"The toughest men should be the most tender because they have learned to live self-controlled lives."

This type of man will also express chivalry. He will recognize his wife as a "weaker vessel," remembering that he is (typically) physically stronger than the woman who is his wife. He practices courtesy and thoughtfulness. There is nothing wrong with a man getting doors, opening jars and lifting boxes for a woman. Toughness and tenderness are not mutually exclusive. The toughest men should be the most tender because they have learned to live self-controlled lives.

This type of man will also enjoy spiritual communion with his wife, showing her honor as a fellow heir of the grace of life, so that his prayers will not be hindered" (1Peter 3:7). Husbands are to live in communion with their wives. More than merely talking to one another, husbands and wives are to touch one another heart-to-heart in deep spiritual communion. They commune together, talk together, and share their hearts with each other. If husbands fail to live in spiritual communion with their wives, God gives them a distinct warning. If a man is not considerate, chivalrous, or in communion with his wife, his prayers will be hindered—literally, cut off. A wrongly ordered marriage closes the windows of heaven to a man's prayers.

Unbreakable, eternal love. Ephesians 5:31–33 says, "For this reason a man shall leave his father and mother and be joined to his wife, and the two shall become one flesh. This mystery is great, but I am speaking with reference to Christ and the church. Nevertheless, each individual among you also is to love his own wife even as himself, and the wife must see to it that she respects her husband."

Once a man is married, the woman he married—and that woman alone—is God's sovereign choice for him, and the covenant with his bride is to be guarded with an unbreakable love. God hates divorce (Malachi 2:14–16), and the one who divorces his spouse is described as a traitor—offensive, deceitful, treacherous, and unfaithful. On the other hand, the man who exercises true biblical headship, never goes back on his promises. He neither breaks his marriage vow, nor backs out of the wedding covenant he made before God, his bride and witnesses. Single men need to build into their thinking, "one life, one wife". In Matthew 19:6, Jesus tells us that a husband and a wife "are no longer two, but one flesh. What therefore God has joined together, let no man separate." God puts couples together. When you attempt to break that bond, you are defying God. Divorce for adultery and desertion is biblically permissible (Matthew 5 and 19, 1 Corinthians 7), but ultimately, God's desire is for the marriage bond to be permanent.

Joyous and intimate love. 1 Corinthians 7:4 says to the Christian husband that his body is not his own but instead belongs to his wife. Proverbs 5:15–19 says that the husband is to be exhilarated, captivated, consumed, and impassioned with the love of his wife.

Once a man is married, his wife should become the standard of beauty for him. The culture should no longer define what beauty is for a Christian husband—he should be able to say honestly from his heart that there is no comparison to his wife's beauty because she is the one God made especially for him. Married men ought to determine in their hearts that their wives are the ideal woman, their personal standard of feminine beauty. The one-flesh relationship a husband experiences with his wife should be so complete that sexual intimacy with her is not only exhilarating but the greatest way they both can express the depth of their love for each other in Christ. The mark of the godly man's life is that he is so committed to sacrificial, purifying, responsible, sensitive, and unbreakable love, that intimate love becomes one of the preeminent expressions of the oneness he shares with his wife. This kind of intimacy does not happen right away. It doesn't come the world's way—cheap and quick—but instead through great sacrifice, maturing in Christ, and growing in a oneness that comes through years of sensitivity, communication, and intentional work.

"Christ's headship is unique, not like what is seen in the world, but a serving, loving leadership which humbly and dependently follows God's Word."

The pursuit of the godly single man is to learn to control his desires so when he gets married he will be able to direct his desires toward his wife alone.

The highest truth for all men who desire to live out God's design is that their ultimate target, their greatest goal, and their best model is our Lord Jesus Himself. He is the perfect model of headship because He is the head of the church. Christ's headship is unique, not like what is seen in the world, but a serving, loving leadership which humbly and dependently follows God's Word (Matthew 20:25–28).

For the young single man, becoming a faithful, committed, and godly spiritual head of his wife does not happen instantly on the wedding day. Instead, it takes years of spiritual commitment through learning the Word, praying, cultivating his giftedness in the church, and walking in the Spirit. And it starts during the years before marriage when he is still single, as he pursues the biblical qualities of manhood which the coming chapters will unfold.

FOR PERSONAL REFLECTION & GROUP DISCUSSION:

1. How would you respond to someone who says male headship is abusive and archaic?

2. Have you ever experienced or practiced bad leadership, and if so, what lessons have you learned from that?

3. Who are some examples of men in your life who love their wives like Christ loved the church?

4. If you are a single man, what are some specific ways you can prepare yourself now to be a godly head of a household in the future?

5. Take some time to pray about your preparation for the future and what you will learn from the rest of this book.

3

LET THE MEN BE GROUNDED
THE FOUNDATION OF BIBLICAL TRUTH

*"But as for you, speak the things which are
proper for sound doctrine."*
TITUS 2:1

Have you heard the story of The Human Fly? An expert rock climber turned showman, he would travel from city to city and scale the tallest skyscrapers. Through advanced publicity, news crews and onlookers would gather in the early morning hours to watch The Human Fly begin his climb upward.

On one occasion, by lunch time, thousands of people had gathered to witness this daredevil's progress. But as they watched, the crowd realized that The Human Fly had stopped. From several hundred feet below they observed him moving to the left and then to the right, but he didn't seem able to navigate a ledge that jetted out from the building. Finally, the Fly apparently figured out what he was going to do. The crowd saw him stretching for something on the ledge above him. Not able to reach it, he jumped up to grasp the unseen object. To their horror, the crowd watched him fall to his death.

Before the body was taken away, the coroner opened the man's clenched fist and found a dusty spiderweb. On The Human Fly's fatal climb, the object that appeared to be solid to him turned out to be only a fragile cobweb.

TODAY'S CRACKED FOUNDATIONS

That story symbolizes the tragedy of the average man in Western civilization today. Society is continually attempting to change the role of a man and redefine the meaning of masculinity. Many businessmen, fathers, husbands, and especially single men find themselves leaping for something solid to hang onto, only to end up with a handful of cobwebs.

THE SHIFTING CULTURE

For centuries, the secular standards were the same. To be admired, a man needed to be physically strong or skilled. He needed to be productive, courageous, wise, and a soldier who battled over his possessions and rights. He needed to be a protector of his spouse, children, and anyone else who was weaker. He also

---

"As a result of the ambiguous and often contradicting cultural demands upon average American men today, many have opted for less-than-best solutions."

---

needed to be the decision-maker for his home, the center of his family, and the captain of his own soul.

Those secular standards are changing. As a result of a major cultural shift and cowardly pulpits that fail to confront it, men are often torn between more traditional expectations and some new ones that are very different. The list of desirable traits for a man is now topped by characteristics like social consciousness, flexibility, tolerance, likability, and some have even suggested, femininity. With the secular definition of manhood being overhauled, it's no wonder many men are confused!

THE WRONG RESPONSES

As a result of the ambiguous and often contradicting cultural demands upon average American men today, many have opted for less-than-best solutions.

Some men have chosen to become the **irresponsible** man. This kind of man keeps his own agenda. He does not want to be tied down to too many commitments. Responsibilities like finances, disciplining children, involvement in church, house repairs, or keeping promises to friends are seen as an irritation and a hindrance to his own personal happiness.

Then there is the **negative** man. This man is strongly opinionated and dogmatic. He frowns more than he smiles, and his speech is full of warnings, rules, routines, and rigid orderliness.

Next is the **distant** man. This type of man may be very often in the presence of his family, but his thoughts are consistently somewhere else. He may be bright and in great demand, but an invisible and often impregnable wall separates such a preoccupied man from his family, who wishes they could break through it.

Another type of man is the **complacent** man, who ends up being absent, passive, or indifferent in his role as a husband and a father.

Last is the **"Peter Pan"** man who refuses to grow up. This is the twenty-to-thirty-year-old who lives with his parents, spends most of his time playing video games while he waits to get offered a bank presidency job—a position for which he is not qualified. He is looking for a company to pay him handsomely simply for showing up, rather than seeking to work hard to advance his career.

The good news for Christian men is that you do not have to fit into any culturally-conditioned category, comply with any human rules, or suffer from any confusion about what kind of single man, husband, or father you have been designed to be. You no longer have to grasp at cobwebs, but instead can find reliable answers in the only foolproof operation manual for manhood—the solid foundation of the Bible.

SOLID FOUNDATIONS IN TITUS 1

The beginning of Titus is a great place to start building an understanding of God's design for both young men and young women (See also Ephesians 5:22–33, Colossians 3:18–19, 1 Peter 3:1–7, and 1 Corinthians 7:25–40). But Titus 2 in particular provides a helpful framework for discussing the most important biblical issues for young men and women because it addresses what they should be now and what they should hope to be in the future. In order to understand Titus chapter 2, it is important to understand the foundation that is laid in Titus 1.

THE IMPORTANCE OF SPIRITUAL HEALTH

Are you as confused as I am about what constitutes a healthy diet? When I was growing up we learned about the four basic food groups. Nowadays, there are at least three times as many! At one time, to "diet" was naturally linked with eating less. Then later came a fad called "the popcorn diet," which suggested a daily intake of 1,200 calories, but with the ability to eat endless popcorn as "filler." This was seriously peddled as a healthy way of living! The Beverly Hills Medical Diet recommended eating only

"Living a physically healthy life is important, of course, but it is not nearly as important as living a spiritually healthy life."

vegetables, grains, and fruit, and not only that, it also recommended "wogging"—a hybrid of walking and jogging. The "rice diet" suggested to an increasingly overweight American populace that the key to losing weight was to eat more like most of the world, by eating rice three times a day, along with a moderate intake of fruit. The "eight-week cholesterol cure" promoted the robust use of oat bran—along with other foods that horses love!

Living a physically healthy life is important, of course, but it is not nearly as important as living a spiritually healthy life. In 1 Timothy 4:7–8 Paul tells his protégé, "Train yourself for the purpose of godliness, for bodily training is only of little profit, but godliness is profitable for all things, since it holds promise for the present life and also for the life to come." In other words, physical health can help a person now, but spiritual health will bless a person forever. Physical health is earth-bound, but spiritual health is heavenly-minded. Physical health is temporally oriented, but spiritual health is eternally based. However, just as with physical health, there is also much confusion about what it means to be spiritually healthy.

There was a time earlier in my life when I was very sick physically. Unfortunately, I did not receive a proper diagnosis of my illness for almost eight weeks. I later learned that I had bronchitis, but by the time I had been accurately diagnosed, my body had become severely weakened, and I found myself susceptible to any disease or virus that was going around at the time. That experience helped me to understand the importance of obtaining a proper diagnosis of my physical condition. It is even more important for Christian young men to have an accurate assessment of their spiritual health, and that is what the book of Titus will provide for us.

Titus too was a ministerial protégé of the apostle Paul. Paul left Titus on the island of Crete for about six months with the job of organizing new believers into churches. Many on the island had turned to Christ through the missionary efforts of Paul and others, so Paul says in Titus 1:5, "For this reason I left you in Crete, that you would set in order what remains and appoint elders in every city as I directed you."

We learn from Titus 1:12 and from history books that Crete was a perverse place filled with untrustworthy and brutish people. In addition to a difficult culture outside the church, troublesome false teachers had invaded the island, injecting errant doctrinal views into the early Cretan church.

Titus himself was a young man, and as Paul instructs him, he admonishes all young men about how to be spiritually healthy. God inspired these words to provide some solid foundations for the further study of Christian manhood in Titus 2.

FOUNDATIONS FOR SPIRITUAL HEALTH

Paul's words to Titus in Chapter 1 contain two key truths that must be understood and practiced before you can even begin to fulfill the roles God has described in Titus 2.

First, in Titus 1:1 we learn that a man must be genuinely saved before he can grow to be God's Man. Here Paul describes believers by referring to "the faith of God's elect and the full knowledge of the truth which is according to godliness." This description is radically different from what is often heard in society and taught in far too few pulpits.

The words "God's elect" remind us of the truth that the entire human race is so utterly sinful that we are hopeless and helpless to do anything to save ourselves. Therefore, we are totally dependent on the mercy of God for our salvation and must trust completely in Christ by the power of the Holy Spirit. Paul explains this further in Titus 3:4–5: "But when the kindness and affection of God our Savior appeared, He saved us, not by works which we did in righteousness, but according to His mercy, through the washing of regeneration and renewing by the Holy Spirit."

God must save you—you can't save yourself. Jesus Christ accomplished your salvation through His perfect sinless life, His substitutionary death on the cross for your sin, and His resurrection from the dead. Your sin has fallen on Christ and, for you to be justified, His righteousness must cover you. Christ took your place so you could exchange all that you are for all that He is. If this is not true of you, then the rest of what Paul has to say is of secondary importance. Salvation is the starting place—the launchpad for biblical manhood.

"Salvation is the starting place—the launchpad for biblical manhood."

Paul's reference in Titus 1:1 to "the full knowledge of the truth which is according to godliness" highlights another important (and often neglected) aspect of what it means to be a true Christian. If you are truly saved, God has regenerated you—caused you to be born again (Titus 3:5 again, cf. John 3:3–7). The Holy Spirit transforms you from the inside out by giving you a new heart that wants to obey God's Word and becomes sorrowful when you fail to do so. Notice Paul's description of the unsaved false teachers in Titus 1:16: "They profess to know God, but by their works they deny Him, being detestable and disobedient and unfit for any good work."

Being a born-again Christian does not merely mean professing

Christ, but also living a uniquely different life from those who do not know Him. You don't work to earn salvation, but once you are saved, you will be known for good works. Why? Because God has given you a heart that desires to obey God's Word. As Romans 6:17 says, "But thanks be to God that though you were slaves of sin, you obeyed from the heart that pattern of teaching to which you were given over."

True salvation results in a heart that desires to obey God's Word. When you are genuinely born again you are regenerated. God has transformed your inner man. All of it is part of God's work in saving you. You must realize you did not choose God and you cannot save yourself—nor can you overcome your sinfulness by your own ability. No, you must cry out to God to open your heart so that you can respond to Christ by turning from your sinfulness in repentance and depending on the work of Christ by faith.

"...you must be interconnected in a local church before you can grow to be God's Man."

The second foundational truth in Titus 1 is that you must be interconnected in a local church before you can grow to be God's Man. Younger men need to emulate older men. All believers need spiritual examples to follow. And by God's design, every Christian needs a community to mature with in order to be more like Christ. Titus 1:5–9 highlights all those ingredients necessary for a young man's growth and for a church's spiritual health—believers gathering under a qualified and functioning team of elders:

For this reason I left you in Crete, that you would set in order what remains and appoint elders in every city as I directed you, namely, if any man is beyond reproach, the husband of one wife, having faithful children, who are not accused of dissipation, or rebellious. For the overseer must be beyond reproach as God's steward, not self-willed, not quick-tempered, not addicted to wine, not pugnacious, not fond of dishonest gain, but hospitable, loving what is good, sensible, righteous, holy, self-controlled, holding fast the faithful word which is in accordance with the teaching, so that he will be able both to exhort in sound doctrine and to reprove those who contradict.

Paul left Titus on the island of Crete to gather the new converts into local churches, assemblies of believers who would function dependently upon the Lord and one another. And for any young man today to grow into his God-designed role, he too needs to be immersed in the ministry and community of a healthy local church made up of born-again believers under a plurality of biblical elders.

One of Paul's goals in appointing elder teams over every church in Crete was to not only ensure that all believers would gather faithfully and regularly in a local church but also that young men would have examples to follow. Like the older women training the younger women (Titus 2:3–5), older men are called to train younger men to live out their roles in the context of a church. This provides young men with models to imitate. And in a local church under an eldership of godly models, it also provides the young man with opportunities to grow as they serve. Every believer is to minister his or her spiritual giftedness in the body of Christ to other members of that same local body. Young men glorify God and grow to be spiritually healthy as they serve (1 Peter 4:10–11). Every young man is to live in community, seeking to fulfill the New Testament "one anothers." The New Testament contains about 40 such commands—love one another, accept one another, admonish one another, be kind to one another, comfort one another, confess your sins to one another, and others. While this may be foreign to many churches today, the personal relationships of Christians in the local church are to be close. The Lord expects each healthy believer to participate in "intentional relationships for the purpose of growth in Christ," which describes the process of discipleship young men are to pursue with other men in the body of Christ. That way each young man is learning how to fulfill the Great Commission and also learning how to become a parent later, since parenting is the process of biblically discipling your children (Matthew 28:18–20).

> # "...a biblically healthy local church is the environment where young men grow into God's men."

God never intended Christians to function independently from one another, so a biblically healthy local church is the environment where young men grow into God's men. It is essential that young Christian men not only attend a church but that they are relationally interconnected with families and men of all ages (not merely their peers), and give, pray, submit and faithfully serve in that local congregation. That kind of commitment is a clear biblical expectation and strongly laid out in Titus chapter one.

SOLID FOUNDATIONS IN TITUS 2

As Paul opens the second chapter of his letter to Titus, he now discusses the character and function of older men, older women, younger women, and our focus in this book, younger men. We could say that Titus 2 is focused on younger men, because the recipient of Paul's letter, Titus, was a young man who needed a foundation of sound doctrine to build his life upon (Titus 2:6-7).

In this passage, Paul gives several indicators of whether or not a young man, or any person, is living a spiritually healthy life.

THE CONTRAST WITH FALSE BELIEVERS

First, spiritually healthy Christians live differently than false Christians. The first word in Titus 2:1 is "but," which is a word of contrast. This contrast is with the ungodly lifestyle of the false teachers exposed in the later verses of Titus 1, and also the negative impact their lifestyle was having on the saints in Crete. So Paul was saying, "Titus, make sure your lifestyle (as a young man) is in contrast to the false teachers and represents Christ well, so that your witness of Him may have a godly impact on the believers around you."

When Paul adds "as for you," the word "you" is emphatic. In the Greek text, it is the first word in the sentence, which gives it a prominent place. Why did Paul want to make sure that Titus sat up and listened to this instruction? He did so because the influence of spiritual leadership is powerful. The lifestyle of the false teachers in Crete was producing ungodly fruit in the lives of the people around them. Similarly, Jesus condemned the Pharisees because of the negative impact they had on people's lives: "Woe to you, scribes and Pharisees, hypocrites, because you travel around on sea and land to make one proselyte; and when he becomes one, you make him twice as much a son of hell as yourselves" (Matthew 23:15).

On the other hand, a positive example is also very powerful. The New Testament is saturated in this truth, as the following examples show: "Brothers, join in following my example, and look for those who walk according to the pattern you have in us" (Philippians 3:17); "Let no one look down on your youthfulness, but show yourself as a model to those who believe in word, conduct, love, faith and purity" (1 Timothy 4:12); "Remember your leaders, who spoke the word of God to you; and considering the result of their conduct, imitate their faith" (Hebrews 13:7); "Be imitators of me, just as I also am of Christ" (1 Corinthians 11:1).

In Titus 2:1, Paul is charging Titus to make sure his lifestyle is unlike the false teachers and in contrast, like Christ. Therefore the lifestyle of Titus was to be uniquely different from the Cretan culture so that it would motivate those around him to also live like Christ. While the false teachers in Crete were living in a way that was impacting the church negatively, Titus (as a young man) was called to live in a way that pointed people to Christ. Unfortunately, not all Christian young men live that way. Why does that happen?

One possible reason is **they are not Christians to begin with**. Just as false teachers confirm the error of their beliefs through engaging in detestable and worthless behavior (Titus 1:10), true believers demonstrate their adherence to the truth of God by living in a godly way. Again, salvation is by grace alone through faith alone, but when a young man is truly saved, his life will produce spiritual fruit, good works, and other aspects of Christlikeness.

When the gospel of Jesus Christ invades a person's life, there will be dramatic lifestyle changes, ethical choices, and moral obligations he will want to pursue. The Bible's clear teaching is that Christians live differently because Jesus Christ has transformed their lives. As Jesus says in Matthew 7:20–23, "So then, you will know them by their fruits. Not everyone who says to Me, 'Lord, Lord,' will enter the kingdom of heaven, but he who does the will of My Father who is in heaven will enter. Many will say to Me on that day, 'Lord, Lord, in Your name did we not prophesy, and in Your name cast out demons, and in Your name do many miracles?' And then I will declare to them, 'I never knew you; depart from me, you who practice lawlessness.'" If a so-called believer continues to practice lawlessness as a way of life, he or she can make no legitimate claim to being a Christian.

The Apostle John said something similar: "Little children, let no one deceive you. The one who does righteousness is righteous, just as He is righteous. By this the children of God and the children of the devil are manifested: everyone who does not do righteousness is not of God, as well as the one who does not love his brother" (1 John 3:7, 10). Simply put, if you are not living differently, you may be deceived and not be a Christian at all. You may not be a real believer but a "make-believer."

> ## "...if you are not living differently, you may be deceived and not be a Christian at all. You may not be a real believer but a 'make-believer.'"

A second reason a young man may not live differently as a Christian is that **he has been negatively influenced by bad company**. In 1 Corinthians 15:33–34, Paul says, "Do not be deceived: 'Bad company corrupts good morals.' Become righteously sober-minded, and stop sinning; for some have no knowledge of God." When he wrote those words to the church at Corinth, Paul was not addressing Christians who were hanging out with sinful unbelievers. Instead, they were hanging out with other so-called Christians who were willfully and intentionally sinning to the point that Paul suggested they may not have known God. In other words, "bad company" was probably a reference to professing Christians who were not really saved.

There should be some caution exercised in living around non-Christians. After all, the unsaved live in sin and do all they can to make their unrepentant lifestyle attractive. But the Bible affirms in 1 Corinthians chapter 5 that there is far greater danger for the believer in living around so-called phony Christians who intentionally remain in a sinful lifestyle. Their influence can erode a true believer's conviction and negatively impact the holiness of the church family. It is extremely dangerous to have a counterfeit living in our midst.

Listen to how Paul warns of this danger:

> *I wrote you in my letter not to associate with sexually immoral people; I did not at all mean with the sexually immoral people of this world, or with the greedy and swindlers, or with idolaters, for then you would have to go out of the world. But now I am writing to you not to associate with any so-called brother if he is a sexually immoral person, or greedy, or an idolater, or a reviler, or a drunkard, or a swindler—not even to eat with such a one (1 Corinthians 5:9–11).*

The primary purpose of the church discipline process outlined in that passage is to bring sinning brothers and sisters to repentance by removing them from the fellowship. But another purpose is to protect the true believers in the church from the bad influence of those who are living in sin and claiming Christ (cf. 1 Corinthians 5:6–7). The danger of relationships with so-called Christians can be far greater than spending time with those who are lost and in need of a Savior.

A third reason a young Christian man might not live a holy life is that **he does not have godly role models in his life**. Remember what Paul taught Titus in the first chapter of his letter—the importance of appointing qualified, mature elders to shepherd and oversee the church. Churches should put their best men in positions of leadership so they can serve as godly models for those who are younger in the faith. Having such biblically qualified elders will impact the church members by spurring them on to live like Christ. Also, the accurate interpretation and sound doctrine taught by godly elders will protect the flock by exposing and rebuking false beliefs and ungodly practices. If a young man is not in a healthy church that is "accurately handling the word of truth," he might not be moved by the Spirit of Truth to live according to truth.

ENCOURAGING OTHERS IN THE TRUTH

In Titus 2:1, another indicator that a young man is living a spiritually healthy life is that he is committed to encouraging others in the truth.

Paul tells Titus to "speak the things which are proper for sound doctrine." When Paul says "speak," the Greek verb is not referring to teaching or preaching. Rather, it refers to ordinary conversation. Moreover, Paul uses the present tense here, which means it should be a continuous action; a lifestyle.

> **"If you are a young man, you should often be speaking with others about sound doctrine."**

So if you are a young man, you should often be speaking with others about sound doctrine. Paul wanted Titus to continually take the initiative to talk to people in the church at Crete about lifestyle choices that would honor the Word of God, make them more like Christ, and distinguish them from the world. Titus was to train others in such a way that would point them to God's character. He was to teach through conversation, discipleship, mentoring, personal involvement, and mutual ministry together, so that people might understand the type of conduct that is befitting to Christian beliefs and consistent with a life transformed by the gospel.

This is why the "Sunday-only" crowd will never experience true spiritual health or aggressive growth. They miss out on church as God designed it, which is much more than Sunday services. God never intended believers to be a part of a church without intimate and consistent fellowship with people in that church community. Sermons are not enough. Sunday worship is not enough. These are, of course, crucial vehicles on the road toward robust Christian maturity, but they're ultimately only a part of what it means to be a flourishing follower of Christ. Strong spiritual health and Christlike character cultivated in men only happens when they are involved in regular conversations related to biblical truth, with a corresponding intent to apply it, to live the truth, and to hold one another accountable to practice the truth every day throughout the week.

For a man to constantly speak the things that are fitting for sound doctrine, he will have to develop relationships with other Christians who are committed to becoming more like Christ. There are many Christians who want to be taught the great doctrines of the faith from the pulpit, but they cringe at the idea of having their rotten attitude confronted over coffee by a fellow brother or sister in Christ. To be a young man who is committed to becoming God's man, a truly masculine man, it will require more than having Christian friends your own age to "hang out with." You will need to develop friendships with older and younger believers in the context of a church family, all of whom are committed to growing in Christlikeness and eager to talk about it.

A "BECOMING" LIFE

A third indicator that a young man, or any person, is living a spiritually healthy life, is when he speaks "the things which are proper for sound doctrine." The Greek word for "proper" means "seemly," "suitable," or "appropriate." In the King James Version, this word is rendered as "becoming."

I have heard there are some clothing patterns that are not very "becoming" on people who have certain body shapes. For example, large people look wider when they wear patterns with horizontal stripes. Additionally, skinny people look even thinner when wearing vertical stripes. But when large people wear vertical stripes and skinny people wear horizontal stripes, it is usually more "becoming."

Paul's point to Titus is this: "Make sure you not only teach people sound doctrine, like I told you to do in Titus 1:9, but also teach them the kind of behavior that is proper, becoming, and suitable for helping them to grow more like Christ." Paul is telling Titus, and all future leaders, to train believers to depend upon the Spirit of God for behavior that is "becoming" to what they have been taught. They cannot do this in their own strength, but Titus exhorts them to live in such a way as is fitting for a Christ-follower. Healthy Christians live in harmony with what they believe.

"Healthy Christians live in harmony with what they believe."

Considering some negative examples can help us better understand the positive truth Paul is communicating in this verse by using the word "proper." It is not "proper" Christlike character, for instance, when a Christian teenager rebels against his or her parents. It is not "proper" for a Christian employee to be lazy at work. It is not "proper" for a Christian husband to fail to live with his wife in an understanding way (1 Peter 3:7) or to fail to love his wife as Christ loved the church (Ephesians 5:25). It is not "proper" for a Christian wife who knows the truth of the gospel to refuse to submit herself to her husband as to the Lord (Ephesians 5:22).

Spiritually healthy Christians are trained in how to live so that the gospel of Jesus Christ is properly adorned by their godly behavior, rather than distorted in an unbecoming fashion.

The grace of God is never to be used as an excuse to do whatever we want—rather it is actually a gift that teaches true believers the importance of obedience. Titus 2:11–12 says, "For the grace of God has appeared, bringing salvation to all men, instructing us that, denying ungodliness and worldly desires, we should live sensibly, righteously and godly in the present age." Remember, however, that living in a "proper" or "becoming" manner does not mean a legalistic adherence to human standards of morality. Paul does not tell Titus to generate a set of rules for Christians to obey so that they appear nice and orderly on the outside.

Rather, to live in a "proper" or "becoming" manner is to live out biblical principles as an act of obedience from a Spirit-transformed and Spirit-empowered heart. These are lifestyle-shifting truths, communicated by God to His people in His Word, that all true Christians want to live out because Jesus has given them a new heart and a desire to please Him. As 2 Corinthians 5:17 says, "If anyone is in Christ, he is a new creation; the old things passed away; behold, new things have come." And Romans 6:17 says, "Though you were slaves of sin, you obeyed from the heart." To obey the Word of God is not legalism. Instead, it is an act of love and worship for our Lord and Master Jesus Christ, who gave up everything to save our souls!

THE FOUNDATION OF SOUND DOCTRINE

The climax of Paul's instruction in Titus 2:1 is when he says to "speak the things which are proper for sound doctrine." What is sound doctrine? The Greek word for "sound" is hygiaino, which means "being healthy, living well." This word is where we get the English word hygiene. The word is used by Jesus in Luke 5:31 when he says, "It is not those who are well who need a physician, but those who are sick." And again, in Luke 7:10, Jesus says that "when those who had been sent returned to the house, they found the slave in good health." In those gospel accounts, the Greek word hugiaino describes a person's physical health. In Titus, however, the word is used five different times, and in each case, it is referring to a person's spiritual health.

The word "doctrine" means teaching or instruction. So, when we put the words "sound" and "doctrine" together, what is being described is the accurate biblical teaching that leads to godly, Christlike living. Sound doctrine leads to spiritually healthy living.

THE IMPORTANCE OF SOUND DOCTRINE

The Bible contains many warnings about what happens when the teaching of sound doctrine is neglected or contradicted. 1 Timothy 6:3–5 contains one of those warnings:

> *If anyone teaches a different doctrine and does not agree with sound words—those of our Lord Jesus Christ—and with the doctrine conforming to godliness, he is conceited, understanding nothing but having a morbid interest in controversial questions and disputes about words, out of which arise envy, strife, slander, evil suspicions, and constant friction between men of depraved mind and deprived of the truth, who suppose that godliness is a means of gain.*

Similarly, 1 Timothy 1:6–7 depicts the confusion caused by a deviation from sound doctrine: "For some, straying from these things, have turned aside to fruitless discussion, wanting to be teachers of the Law, even though they do not understand either what they are saying or the matters about which they make confident assertions." And 1 Timothy 1:10 contrasts those who adhere to sound doctrine and those who engage in various forms of licentious and ungodly living, including "sexually immoral persons, for homosexuals, for kidnappers, for liars, for perjurers, and whatever else is contrary to sound teaching."

Sound doctrine is right teaching that results in righteous living. Sound doctrine is correctly interpreted biblical truth that results in increasingly Christlike behavior. Sound doctrine is not ear-tickling "truth" that merely tells us what we want to hear (2 Timothy 4:3–4). If you are sitting under ear-tickling teaching, rather than sound doctrinal teaching, you are being served diseased meat, which ultimately is going to make you sick rather than sound—you will be unhealthy spiritually and not vibrant for Christ. After praying for discernment and direction, plus meeting with your leaders, you may need to humbly change churches.

SOUND DOCTRINE AND YOUNG MEN

Paul had already taught Titus how an elder needs to approach the teaching of God's Word: "Holding fast the faithful word which is in accordance with the teaching, so that he will be able both to exhort in sound doctrine and to reprove those who contradict" (Titus 1:9). Young men need to be accurate and humble in their conclusions about Scripture, not unresolved and haughty. What do I mean by that? For young men who follow the example of godly elders, this means they should labor to be exact, "in accordance with the teaching"—to teach the biblical author's intended meaning.

Young men have a propensity to keep their options open theologically, which is often a cover for laziness and an unwillingness to study the Bible. They will read a blog article instead of spending time in the pages of the Word itself. They will unthinkingly follow a favorite teacher or podcaster instead of striving to understand the author's intent in the text. They will default to an "open position" instead of wrestling with the Scriptures to find the answers. But Paul says we should be "holding fast the faithful word which is in accordance with the teaching" (Titus 1:9).

Young men also need to embrace the priority of living the truth. Often, they are caught up in debate and controversy without any thought of being holy and becoming more like Christ. They often want to appear scholarly by debating theology, without an accurate understanding of Scripture and diligent application to their own lives.

Sound doctrine, however, is healthy truth that is lived out. Titus chapter 2 itself is evidence of this fact: It is about sound doctrine (verse 1), and yet, it is also filled with discussions of Christlike character to be lived out in everyday life (verses 2–10). This is the right path for the young man to be treading. It is wise to invest more time living the truth than debating the latest theological controversy.

Our Lord Jesus Christ is the ultimate model when it comes to God's Word and sound doctrine. He continually manifested a love for, trust in, and obedience to the Scriptures. When tempted Himself, He said to Satan, "It is written, 'Man shall not live on bread alone, but on every word that proceeds out of the mouth of God.'" (Matthew 4:4). After His resurrection, He said to the disciples on the Emmaus road, "'O foolish ones and slow of heart to believe in all that the prophets have spoken! Was it not necessary for the Christ to suffer these things and to enter into His glory?' Then beginning with Moses and with all the prophets, He interpreted to them the things concerning Himself in all the Scriptures" (Luke 24:25–27). And when pouring out His heart in prayer to the Father, the Son says this in John 17:17: "Sanctify them by the truth; Your word is truth." Simply stated, for a young man to grow to be a godly man, he must become a man of the Word.

Let the Word be your guide. Read the Word, meditate on the Word, memorize the Word, listen to the Word, learn to study the Word. Cultivate in your heart a love for truth, and saturate your mind with it. Then in dependence on the Holy Spirit, seek to be a doer of the Word in every way.

SOUND DOCTRINE AND GRACE

Young men are often warriors for truth. That is good, but those who are zealous over sound doctrine can often lack love and grace. Our Lord Jesus was "full of grace and truth" (John 1:14). Because Christ is our ultimate example, you and I should speak the truth in love (Ephesians 4:15) and demonstrate grace in our speech (Ephesians 4:29).

You should live in light of God's grace, living worthy of the salvation you have been given, not only in your speech but in all areas of your life. This is a primary point Paul makes in his letter to Titus. Young men should always pursue living the truth in light of the "grace of God" (Titus 2:11), which has been shown to us through Christ and is "instructing us that, denying ungodliness and worldly desires, we should live sensibly, righteously and godly in the present age" (Titus 2:12).

God's men seek to live godly lives—spiritually healthy lives—because they seek to live each day remembering what Jesus did for them in bearing their sin, taking their punishment, shedding His blood, and dying in their place. They realize Christ took all the Father's righteous wrath for their sin upon Himself, then rose from the dead and ascended into heaven.

God's men remember they did not seek God, but rather God sought them, called them to Himself, gave them the faith to believe, granted them forgiveness, a new heart, heaven and an eternal inheritance as co-heirs with Christ. To live godly lives in response to these truths is not an act of repaying a debt to the Lord, but instead is actually an act of worship. We should each seek to please Him and demonstrate our thankfulness to Him. The grace of God is what motivates His children to lead spiritually healthy lives. So the grace of God should be reflected in an abundant life lived by God's Word and sound doctrine.

FOR PERSONAL REFLECTION & GROUP DISCUSSION:

1. Have you seen or experienced confusion about what God designed men to be? What are some examples?

2. What are some reasons that spiritual disciplines are more important than physical exercise, as Paul says in 1 Timothy 4:7–8?

3. What are some evidences of true conversion mentioned in this chapter (and/or in the book of 1 John)? How can you "examine yourself" based on them (2 Corinthians 13:5)?

4. Why are good relationships with other believers in a local church so important, and what are some specific, practical ways that you can cultivate more of them?

5. Compare and contrast the benefits of different tools (e.g., blog posts vs. Bible commentaries) when studying spiritual and scriptural issues. Why might some tools be better than others?

4

LET THE MEN BE MATURE
THE GOAL OF GODLINESS

*"Older men are to be temperate, dignified,
sensible, sound in faith, in love, in perseverance."*
TITUS 2:2

How can you tell when you are getting older? You know you're getting older when most of your dreams are reruns. Or when you sit down in a rocking chair and can't get it moving. Or when your mind is making commitments that your body cannot keep. Or when everything hurts, and what doesn't hurt, doesn't work! Inside every older person, they say, is a younger person who is wondering what happened.

GOD'S PERSPECTIVE ON OLDER MEN

Everyone struggles, to some degree, with becoming—or being—older. Why? It becomes harder to live with a body that is in decline, and we live in a society that worships youth. We are all familiar with advertising that tries to convince us our gray hair can be turned back imperceptibly to its "natural color"—presumably because gray is labeled "unnatural." Something must be done about those horrid age spots! Wrinkles must be made smooth!

We hear the not-so-subtle message being communicated: being young is great and being old is bad. The results of this type of youth-elevated thinking is devastating. This mindset contributes to the sad reality that we are becoming less and less mature as a culture. In contrast, the elderly, with all their knowledge, wisdom, experience, and stability, are increasingly being ignored and dismissed as irrelevant.

THE BLESSING OF OLDER MEN

While our society has an increasingly diminished view of older people, God does not. Consider what Scripture teaches. According to Proverbs 16:31, "Gray hair is a crown of beauty; it is found in the way of righteousness." Proverbs 17:6 says, "Grandchildren are the crown of old men, and the beauty of sons is their fathers." And Proverbs 20:29 adds, "The honor of young men is their strength, and the majesty of old men is their gray hair."

Each of those passages teaches that God highly values the seasoned people around us. This is why, in Titus 2, Paul describes the qualities of godly older men before he addresses the younger men. In Titus 2:2, he says, "Older men are to be temperate, dignified, sensible, sound in faith, in love, in perseverance."

Titus 1 indicates that a church that is spiritually healthy (and therefore attractive to the lost) will have a plurality of godly leaders—qualified elders who can exhort with accurate teaching and refute those who are not sound in doctrine. Now in Titus 2, Paul teaches Titus that a healthy and attractive church will be made up of believers who are pursuing their God-given design.

The first group of believers Paul discusses are the older men. But remember that Paul's words are addressed to a younger man,

Titus, so they do not only apply to the older men. Principles drawn from this text tell us about the maturity and character that younger men should make their spiritual targets. These are the qualities a godly young man should pursue, with the goal of becoming a Christlike older man in the future.

WHAT DOES "OLDER" MEAN?

It's crucial to our understanding of this passage that we address the question of what—or who—is an "older" man? The Bible is not definitive on who is "older." In ancient Greek literature, the word was sometimes used of men as young as fifty. Some studies indicate that the average lifespan in Crete when Paul wrote Titus was in the early forties. But in 1 Timothy 5:9, Paul says, "A widow is to be put on the list only if she is not less than sixty years old." So how old is "older"? Is it Forties? Fifties? Sixties? Putting all the evidence together, it appears that men in their mid-forties and above would qualify as "older men."

As interesting as that question is, the primary emphasis in this passage is not on chronological age, but on spiritual maturity. The two categories tend to overlap to some degree, of course, because we would expect a reasonable amount of time to elapse in a man's life before he becomes a very mature Christian. The main factor in spiritual growth is not time, however, but how well a person submits to the truths of Scripture and lives by the

> **"...your spiritual strength is not determined by how long you have been in the boat, but by how hard you have been pulling on the oars."**

power of the Spirit. So a young man can accelerate his spiritual growth by constantly responding to the Spirit of God according to the Word of God. To use an illustration, your spiritual strength is not determined by how long you have been in the boat, but by how hard you have been pulling on the oars. Some Christian young men are more spiritually mature than some older men, simply because they have been living dependently upon the Spirit and obediently to God's Word as a way of life.

CHARACTERISTICS OF SPIRITUAL MATURITY

Directed by the Spirit of God, the Apostle Paul gave his protégé a list of some essential qualities that older men desperately needed to develop. These qualities, which were modeled by our Lord Jesus and Paul himself, also provide a target for every young man to aim at and look for in the lives of older godly men. So let's explore the list from Titus 2.

"TEMPERATE"

When Paul tells Titus that older men should be temperate, the Greek word he uses describes a life of moderation—a balanced life. The word comes from a root that means "sober," which refers to abstaining from drunkenness in its literal sense; "sober-minded" when used figuratively. Elders are to be temperate (1 Timothy 3:2), women who assist deacons are to be temperate (1 Timothy 3:11), and as Paul tells Titus here, older men are to be temperate. Being temperate means a life that is watchful, alert, guided by clear thinking, and remaining steady in the storm. Godly older men are the experienced sailors on the ship of faith.

Most of us suffer from the peril of the swinging pendulum of life. We tend to react, rather than act. The pendulum swings in one direction, then when we become aware of it, we react and end up swinging to the other extreme. When you are younger, sometimes it seems like the only time you are truly balanced is when you are leaving one extreme and swinging toward the opposite extreme, and on the way you briefly hit the middle ground of balance.

Older men are called to live balanced lives that are demonstrably different from unbelievers, as well as less mature believers. A spiritually mature man is not out of control and is not confused as to what is important. Rather he is clear-headed in his thinking and not over-indulgent in his eating, drinking, pleasure-seeking, sleeping, recreation, gaming, hobbies, or downtime.

Young men will think nothing of spending six hours playing video games into the wee hours of the morning, even though they have to work, go to school, or serve in some ministry commitments where they would benefit from a good night's sleep. An older, temperate man will go to bed so that he is well rested and ready to fulfill his obligations and commitments.

"DIGNIFIED"

Paul says that older men should live a life worthy of respect. The spiritually mature man is "dignified." He has earned the respect of others (dignified) because he is not flippant, shallow, directionless, or irresponsible, but in dependence on God he has grown to be serious, noble, purposeful, and committed. That does not mean mature men are never lighthearted or fun, but they know what they believe, and trust in the Spirit of God to live what they believe. Those who are dignified take the Lord very seriously, but do not take themselves seriously at all. This is the kind of person who is able to laugh at himself, laugh with others, and otherwise live a joyful life because of a deep and personal intimacy with the Savior who calls him to a serious mission in the midst of a hostile world.

The root of the word translated "dignified" in this passage is often used in relation to worship, which helps us to understand what Paul meant. All of life—not just a Sunday morning church service—should be an expression of worship for the Christian. A mature man does not divide up his life by thinking, that is for

Jesus and this is for me. Instead, he recognizes that everything is for Christ. To live is Christ. When an everyday person is in the presence of someone who holds a high office, he or she will act differently—namely, more politely and seriously. A dignified man is one who lives in the presence of our King and our Master, Jesus Christ, all the time. He knows who is in charge and who is not.

A dignified man is serious about eternal things. This does not mean he is a gloomy killjoy. However, he is convinced that though many people are headed to eternal bliss in heaven, there are even more headed for eternal torment in hell, and he is gravely concerned about that. He is not one to joke about people going to hell, nor is he one to find pleasure or entertainment in immorality, vulgarity, or anything else that is sinful. He is not one who laughs at what is tragic or at the expense of others. He loves the things that God loves and grieves over the things that grieve the Lord.

Additionally, a dignified man is less and less attracted to the pleasures of this life. Older, spiritually mature followers of Christ have lived long enough to see good friends and family members experience serious misfortune, suffer great pain, and perhaps die at an early age. Dignified men can clearly see the deceptions of this sinful world and the inability of material things to give any lasting satisfaction. They understand what really matters and what really lasts. Godly older men see life through eternal lenses. They know what is eternal and what is not, and have seen and lived the truth of Christ's words in Matthew 6:33: "Seek first His kingdom and His righteousness, and all these things will be added to you." For all those reasons, dignified men are worthy of respect.

"SENSIBLE"

Spiritually mature older men live sensible lives. The word "sensible" represents a major theme of Titus, as it appears four times in this short letter. Being sensible was not only a major issue on the island of Crete during Titus' ministry there, but is also a major issue today—it is a missing quality in the lives of young men especially, but also in many older men. In the Greek language, the word "sensible" is built upon two root words. The first root word means "to save" and the second means "the mind." Putting these concepts together tells us that being "sensible" is to live controlled in one's thinking, which ultimately results in biblically wise living. Spiritually mature men think before they act.

So, **the sensible man is focused in his thinking**. He is able to take "every thought captive to the obedience of Christ," as Paul commanded the Corinthians to do as they were struggling with errant belief systems (2 Corinthians 10:5). Sensible men depend upon the Holy Spirit in order to live out Philippians 4:8: "Finally, brothers, whatever is true, whatever is dignified, whatever is right, whatever is pure, whatever is lovely, whatever is commendable, if there is any excellence and if anything worthy of praise, consider these things." The mature older man focuses his thoughts on the things of God. He disciplines his thinking. He says no to tempting thoughts. He says no to lustful thinking. His goal is to think only about what is true, dignified, right, pure, lovely, and so forth. He may even verbally say, "Lord, I am not going to allow my thoughts to dwell on that line of thinking, but think the way You want me to."

Not only does the mature believer refuse to waste his life away with useless thoughts, but he also focuses his thinking upon God's character and God's cause. He spends more time reading or listening to edifying Christian content than he does watching mindless secular entertainment. He is reading the Bible (which is absolutely true) more than he is watching or reading the news (which is not always true). He is a man whose thoughts are being shaped by godly influences. In conversation, he is discussing ideas more than he is gossiping about people. He is not following the world's ways of speculating or spreading questionable or needless information. He remembers the teaching of Proverbs 10:19: "When there are many words, transgression is unavoidable, but he who holds back his lips has insight." When he does open his mouth, he seeks to have his conversation filtered by the truth of the Word, right theology, God's character, and the mission of the church.

"The mature man is not in bondage to his desires...whether they be money, food, sex, sports, hobbies, video games, or other habits."

Also, **the sensible man is able to control his appetites**. Over his years of learning and growing, the godly older man has developed the strength of mind which allows him to govern his passions and keep them in their proper place. The mature man is not in bondage to his desires, impulses, or passions—whether they be money, food, sex, sports, hobbies, video games, or other habits. Contrary to cultural expectations, he does not experience a "mid-life crisis," because he has trained himself to be sensible. He seeks to have only the Spirit of God and the Word of God empower, control, and direct him.

When viewed together, these three words—temperate, dignified, and sensible—describe a man who is respectable in the sight of others. He is a man that other men will trust. So it is crucial that older men manifest these qualities, and every young man should strive to grow in them.

CHARACTERISTICS OF GODLINESS

Next, Paul tells Titus that older men are to be "sound in faith, in love, in perseverance." Whereas "temperate," "dignified," and "sensible" relate to a man's maturity, "sound in faith, in love, in perseverance" refers to his godliness. In the Greek text of Titus, the word "sound" is a participle connected to all three of the words following—"faith," "love," and "perseverance." Remember, the Greek word for "sound" means "being healthy, living well," and when the words "sound" and "doctrine" appear together, they describe accurate biblical teaching that leads to godly Christlike living. Also, the present-tense form of the verb Paul uses here (for "sound") indicates that a godly older man should continually live in such a manner—24/7, not just occasionally.

SOUND IN FAITH

To say that the godly, mature man is "sound in faith" means that he has healthy and biblically rooted doctrinal convictions. Older men know what they believe, and their doctrinal convictions are in harmony with the Word of God rather than the latest book, podcast, politician, blogger, public speaker, or favorite author. Mature men are men of conviction. They are men who stand for truth. They realize if you do not stand for something, you are prone to fall for anything.

Many men today find themselves on shaky ground. Very few are willing to speak up and say another person's actions or beliefs are in violation of Scripture. But spiritually mature men are ready and willing to speak the truth, share the gospel, speak out against sin, correct theological error, and lovingly point out when fellow Christians are off track in their thinking. They do so, saturated with grace, but never compromising truth, just like Christ - who is "full of grace and truth" (John 1:14).

A godly man will speak the truth graciously. He is not passive about truth, but passionate about truth. He is able to sort out the essential from the trivial and articulate healthy convictions about the basic truths of the Christian faith.

To say that a spiritually mature man is "sound in faith" also means that he has an intimate relationship with Jesus Christ. He has a living and committed relationship with the Lord. He is fully reliant upon and confident in Christ. He trusts in God's sovereign plans. The older man's passion is to finish strong for Christ. He does not fight for his faith only when it is convenient, but instead, like Paul in 2 Timothy 4:2, he is willing to fight the battles of faith to the very end of his life. He seeks to live every moment of his life for God's glory and does not give in to the world's view of "retirement," where some devote their twilight years to things like motorhomes, golf, and travel instead of the Great Commission.

SOUND IN LOVE

Not only is the mature man "sound in faith," but he is also sound "in love." He regularly demonstrates a tender, truthful, and sacrificial love. He is not only a man of conviction but also a man of compassion. One of the greatest dangers associated with aging as a Christian is the possible drift toward criticism and fault-finding. Sometimes sympathy fades away with age. For other men, their heart becomes hardened and they don't respond with grace.

The man who is sound in love has a heart of Spirit-generated love (Romans 5:5) that results in a life of sacrifice. He resists the temptation some older believers face to become increasingly self-centered in their later years. Paul wanted Titus to remind older men to continue to cultivate a heart that loves to give and will seek out those most in need of care. It's been said, "a mark of spiritual maturity occurs when a believer takes off the bib and puts on an apron." Immature believers, like infants and toddlers, expect

> " '...a mark of spiritual maturity occurs when a believer takes off the bib and puts on an apron.' "

others to meet all their needs. Mature saints have learned to put on aprons for the joy of serving others.

Being sound in love also includes being a man of truth. To be sound in love does not mean that older men should grow to be sentimental, artificial, or otherwise sloppy with love. Rather, the godly older man will have a disciplined, action-oriented, truth-directed sacrificial love, where he has learned to confront in love and be patient with others when working out issues (Philippians 1:9–11).

SOUND IN PERSEVERANCE

Last, the godly older man is sound "in perseverance." The word "perseverance" means endurance, patience, and steadfastness. As we grow older, we normally lose our strength in various ways, causing us to feel hesitant and unsure. So Paul reminds older saints to be steadfast. As a man approaches the label 'senior', with life's increasing infirmities, disappointments, and sometimes loneliness, it is crucial for him to develop this characteristic of godliness. Such perseverance and endurance is not stubborn endurance but steady consistency. When the going gets tough, it will be the godly older men who say to us all, "God will show us a way—He always has!"

Practically speaking, what target does Titus 2 offer the young man to aim for, as he seeks to grow in perseverance?

First, the man who desires to be God's man will **stand strong under pressure**. The Greek word for "perseverance" paints a great picture of how God wants us to live—it means to "remain under." The man who will make a difference for Christ is the man who will remain faithful under the weight of a trial until God releases him (James 1:2–4). The young man who desires to become a godly older man will refuse to complain, and will not try to escape. He will bear the trials and afflictions of life with patience, even thankfulness, imitating the example of older men. He values relationships with brothers and sisters who have been tempered by trials and have developed character as tough as steel. The young man depends on God's Spirit, follows God's Word, and trusts in God's character in order to emerge a steadfast conqueror over the troubles of life.

A godly young man should also **manifest an unbreakable commitment** to Christ. The Greek word for "perseverance" was used in military contexts for holding up courageously under fire. It speaks of an ability to endure a battle even though bullets are flying all around you. Perseverance means to remain steadfast without compromise. The ultimate test in the Christian life is not simply your entrance into the race, but your endurance throughout the race. And the godly young man starts early by developing an unswerving commitment to Jesus Christ no matter what challenges lie before him. His goal is to become a faithful, no-excuses, dependable young man.

"The ultimate test in the Christian life is not simply your entrance into the race, but your endurance throughout the race."

Our Lord Jesus is the ultimate model of faith, love, and perseverance. In the midst of the incredible physical and spiritual agony on the cross, the Lord cried out, "Father, forgive them; for they do not know what they are doing" (Luke 23:34). All throughout His earthly ministry, Christ would live out the words He would ultimately say in Gethsemane: "Yet not as I will, but as You will" (Matthew 26:39). He trusted the Father and persevered through the greatest test the world has ever known. It is Christ who shows us how to sacrifice in love, how to live dependent by faith, and how to endure with perseverance.

MORE IMPLICATIONS FOR YOUNG MEN

Young men should not only make these essential qualities of older godly men a target to aim at and pursue, but the list should also point them toward developing relationships with older brothers whose lives are marked by them.

RELATIONSHIPS BETWEEN OLDER AND YOUNGER MEN

As older men seek to become spiritual examples to the entire church, young men should be spending time with them and asking questions. Discipleship can be defined as intentional relationships for the purpose of growth in Christ, and young men need to seek this out from older men, just as Titus learned from Paul. The qualities mentioned in Titus 2:2 are not only required of older men, but they are also desperately needed in the rest of the church, especially in young men. The church needs the example of older men to show younger men the way, and young men must also pursue close relationships with older godly men in order to learn from them and model their behavior. When furniture is new, you talk about it; when it is used, you are comfortable with it; but when it becomes an antique, it is highly valued. Like antiques, older godly men and women must be treasured in your church and in your life.

This verse challenges younger men to honor the older men in their lives. Even though modern western culture honors seniors less and less, younger Christian men are not to follow the ways of the world but the commands of God. And God commands the younger men to revere and respect older men. Both the Old and New Testaments teach that older men and women are to be treated with special respect by those who are younger. Not only are children told to honor their parents (an Old Testament command, which was punishable by death if violated), but older men are to be treated with respect even when they speak error or make a mistake (1 Timothy 5:1).

This verse also teaches both young and old that it is important to link up with other generations in the body of Christ. Titus 2:4, for instance, tells the older women to train the younger women, while 1 Peter 5:5 tells younger men to rank themselves under the older men. We need each other, and by God's design, older and younger should not always be separated in the church but should be interconnected in many meaningful ways.

MAKING THE MOST OF YOUR TIME

Titus 2:2 encourages younger men to let their time work for God, and if they do not, their time will work against them. Likewise, Ephesians 5:15–16 challenges all believers: "Therefore look carefully how you walk, not as unwise but as wise, redeeming the time, because the days are evil." Whether you are young or old, if you have lived your life up to this point for yourself, the time is now to correct your ways and begin investing yourself into the lives of others, including those from a different generation. If you are already an older man, you should pursue these qualities because failing to do so will result in a poor witness, loss of blessing, and missed opportunity to give glory to God. If you are a younger man, know that you will grow old faster than you realize, so set the qualities listed in Titus 2:2 as a clear target to aim at while you are still young.

In the last chapter of Ecclesiastes, we are told, "Remember also your Creator in the days of your youth, before the evil days happen and the years draw near in which you will say, 'I have no delight in them'" (Ecclesiastes 12:1). As we grow older, change can be harder to accept. We may become increasingly disillusioned and feel like life is unsatisfying and less fulfilling. If we are not careful, we can develop into selfish 'creatures of habit.' And the longer a habit is practiced, the more deeply entrenched it becomes in our life.

For a Christian, old age should mean greater love for God, greater love for God's people, and a greater passion for God's purposes. The church should highly value those who have spent many years walking with the Lord in the study of God's Word and in service to His church. The body of Christ is greatly blessed when it has mature believers who can say, along with Paul, "I have fought the good fight, I have finished the course, I have kept the faith" (2 Timothy 4:7).

FOR PERSONAL REFLECTION & GROUP DISCUSSION:

1. What are some ways that our culture elevates youth and denigrates old age?

2. How should Christians address that problem?

3. How can a man be lighthearted or fun yet still be "dignified" (as defined in this chapter)?

4. How sound (or spiritually healthy) are you in faith, love, and perseverance? Rate yourself from 1 to 10 in each category and identify at least one area of growth in all three.

5. What are some practical ways that older and younger Christian men can develop relationships with each other?

5

LET THE MEN BE SENSIBLE
THE STABILITY OF A SOUND MIND

"Likewise urge the younger men to be sensible."
TITUS 2:6

Raynald III, a fourteenth-century duke in what is now Belgium, was grossly overweight. Raynald was commonly called by his nickname, Crassus, which means "fat" in Latin. After a violent quarrel, Raynald's younger brother Edward led a successful revolt against him. Edward captured Raynald but did not kill him. Instead, he built a room around Raynald in the castle and promised him he could regain his title and property as soon as he was able to leave the room.

This would not have been difficult for most people since the room had several windows and a door of near-normal size. Plus, none of the windows nor the door were locked or barred. The problem was Raynald's size. To regain his freedom, all he needed to do was lose weight.

But Edward knew his older brother well, so each day he sent him a variety of delicious foods. Instead of dieting his way out of prison, Raynald grew larger and remained in the room for ten years. He was not released until Edward died in battle.

The real issue was not Raynald's size, of course, but his lack of motivation and self-control, which all started with the thoughts in his mind about food, life in general, and even God.

Unfortunately, you don't have to be an overweight fourteenth-century monarch to be imprisoned by your appetites. Anyone can live without self-control over his thoughts or actions.

We are all aware, on some level, of how difficult it can be to exercise self-governance, relying on the Spirit of God and prioritizing the Word of God over our own desires. Just like Raynald was enslaved by his appetite, every young man has something that competes with the Lord for control of his life.

As young men experience the freedoms of life after high school, those same freedoms can also require more discipline. Young adult males typically experience the intense increase of their sexual drives; they make more choices about how to use their money and time; their home responsibilities decrease; and the world's influences become louder and stronger. In these early years of manhood, Christian men need to cultivate the quality of sensibility. To be sensible is more than being self-controlled, thinking correctly, and acting wisely, as we will see. Becoming sensible was desperately needed in the church at Crete and is desperately needed in our lives today.

THE IMPORTANCE OF BEING SENSIBLE

Titus 2:6 says, "Likewise urge the younger men to be sensible." As stated earlier, the term "younger men" does not refer only to teenagers or college-aged men but even men in their early forties. Therefore, Titus 2:6 and the following verses represent God's priorities for men in all those age groups. Married women should encourage their husbands and sons to pursue these traits, and single women should put them on their list of qualities to look for in their future husbands.

WHY IS "SENSIBLE" MENTIONED FIRST?

The first quality Paul mentions when he addresses young men is "sensible." This was the most important quality for young men to develop in first-century Crete, and I believe it is for today as well. In Chapter 4, we learned that a sensible older man is one who exercises self-control, especially in his thinking. In this chapter, because this quality is so foundational and important, we will go deeper and further into our understanding and application of sensibility.

Too many men today act like they have lost their minds—from making bad decisions to behaving recklessly; from indifference to dangerous risk-taking; from frustrating silence to thoughtless words; from not providing to overspending; from arrogant self-righteousness to hypocritical ungodly living.

I heard a story about a man who was hit on his head at work. The blow he received was so severe that he was knocked unconscious for an extended period of time. His family, believing he was dead, called the funeral home and asked the local undertaker to pick him up at the hospital, which he did. Early the following morning, the man suddenly woke up while lying in a casket. Confused, he blinked several times, looked around, trying to put the whole story together. Then he spoke to himself, "If I'm alive, what in the world am I doing in this soft, satin-filled box? And if I'm dead, why do I have to go to the bathroom?"

The sensible man is never disconnected and removed from life, only to wake up disoriented in a spiritual coma.

The sensible man seeks to avoid being enslaved by habits, vices, or his own weaknesses. He does not allow his desires, emotions, lusts, expectations, hopes, or anger to control him. He remains spiritually alert for himself, his family, and his friends. He makes

> # "The sensible man is never disconnected and removed from life, only to wake up disoriented in a spiritual coma."

certain it is God's Word which guides all his steps. He is not one to go off the rails when things go bad, to engage in impulsive purchases, to fight over non-essentials or preferential matters, or to otherwise act without thinking. A young man cannot mature into a godly man, fulfill his God-given role, or be used greatly by our King unless he cultivates a consistent pattern of sensibility.

WHY IS "SENSIBLE" MENTIONED SO MANY TIMES?

Sensibility is the most repeated specific quality in the book of Titus. Paul mentions sensibility, in some form, four times in the first two chapters alone! Paul tells elders, older men, younger women, young men, and all believers that they should live sensibly in the midst of an unthinking generation. That idea is repeated often in this particular letter because the Christian community on Crete battled with a society that actually encouraged their citizens to live without thinking. We see this in Titus 1:12–14: "One of themselves, a prophet of their own, said, 'Cretans are always liars, evil beasts, lazy gluttons.' This testimony is true. For this reason reprove them severely so that they may be sound in the faith, not paying attention to Jewish myths and commandments of men who turn away from the truth." Simply stated, the Cretans were living without sense.

When Paul writes in Titus 2:6, "Likewise urge the younger men to be sensible," he is essentially saying this to Titus: "Just as you have encouraged the older men and women, you now need to urge [lit. beg or plead] the younger men to pursue living sensible lives." Note, however, that verse 6 does not sit in a vacuum. Rather, it is connected to Titus 2:7, which says: "In all things show yourself to be a model of good works." The instruction in verse 6 is better understood together with what follows in verse 7. When Paul says "in all things" in verse 7, that phrase is grammatically connected to the charge in verse 6. Thus, Paul's exhortation to young men is literally to "live sensibly in all things." Sensibility must be applied to every single area of our lives.

Not living as a sensible man can be incredibly destructive. In fact, it was the lack of this very quality that destroyed Alexander the Great. Alexander had everything a man could desire. His body was a spectacular specimen of masculine perfection. He married the most beautiful princesses of the known world. He was the son of Philip of Macedon, a great Greek king, and raised in a palace with Aristotle himself as a companion and teacher. Yet, Alexander the Great died at age 33 from alcoholism and venereal disease. He conquered the known world but never conquered himself. His private life was lived without sensibility. Sensibility is necessary to think rightly, control yourself, make wise decisions, set the best goals, and exercise true spiritual leadership. Without it, one's life will fall apart.

THE MEANING OF "SENSIBLE"

In chapter 4 "sensible" was defined as living controlled in one's thinking, but since it is such an important quality, it is worth looking at other biblical passages that provide helpful context and insights into the term.

A form of this word is used in 1 Peter 4:7: "The end of all things is at hand; therefore, be of sound thinking and sober spirit for the purpose of prayer." The word translated "sound thinking" in that verse is the same word Paul uses for "sensible" in Titus 2:6. Sensibility includes the skill of making good decisions based on logical thinking about issues so we can pray with wisdom.

A similar passage is Romans 12:3: "For through the grace given to me I say to each one among you not to think more highly of himself than he ought to think; but to think so as to have sound thinking, as God has allotted to each a measure of faith." Again, the word here for "sound thinking" is the same as "sensible" in Titus 2:6. The sensible man is realistic and humbly honest about himself and his abilities.

Translators sometimes use "sound" in translating this Greek word because one of its root words means "safe." So we could say that the thinking of a godly young man is "safe and sound," and that he is "of sound mind." These terms are also related to the idea of being healthy, so sensibility includes assessing your spiritual state accurately and making beneficial decisions for yourself and others. Young men can be idealistic, but as they mature, a healthy dose of realism should accompany their idealism. A young man needs to be able to see life through the lens of God's Word and sound theology (the most accurate lenses), so he will be able to see things as they really are.

> **"A young man needs to be able to see life through the lens of God's Word and sound theology (the most accurate lenses), so he will be able to see things as they really are."**

2 Corinthians 5:13 says, "For if we are out of our mind, it is for God, or if we are of right mind, it is for you." The word Paul uses here for "right mind" is the same word he uses in Titus 2:6

for "sensible." To be "sensible," then, means to have a healthy thought-life, to be able to decide what is best for yourself and others for whom you are responsible. The sensible man knows how to determine and follow God's will for His life. He seeks God's will as expressed in God's Word and pursues God's wisdom by saturating himself in the Word and depending on the Spirit to lead him in applying the truth to every life situation.

Another usage of this Greek word is found in the gospel accounts of the man possessed by a legion of demons. Mark 5:15 says, "And they came to Jesus and observed the demon-possessed man sitting down, clothed and in his right mind, the very man who had the 'legion'; and they became frightened." The word the gospel writers use for "in his right mind" is the same word Paul uses for "sensible" in Titus 2:6. To be sensible is to be a young man who is not skewed in his thinking. He is not dominated by bad influences like unbelieving college professors, bloggers, entertainers, or other purveyors of worldly philosophies. He is also not a slave to his own ideas or desires.

The sensible young man is not someone whose goals and dreams have no basis in reality. Rather, he understands who he is and what he can do, and seeks to use all his abilities for God's glory. He is not given to the extremes of pride or false humility. A sensible man does not lose control of his faculties or behave wildly without thinking. Plus, he never relinquishes his mind to outside influences. He exercises wise judgment and avoids excesses in every area of his life by practicing Holy Spirit-empowered self-control over his thinking and lifestyle.

We've all witnessed on television musical competition contestants who think that he or she is a great singer. Then at the end of their performance, one of the judges is blunt with their critique, informing them of their lack of talent. In response, the sad-voiced contestant becomes indignant. Why? Because their family and friends informed them over the course of their life, that they were a star in the making. That singer is an example of someone who lacks a sensibility. Their goals or dreams have no basis in reality. God wants you to rightly assess how He has made you and live accordingly.

That all may seem like a tall order, especially if you have not been committed to Christ or practicing good habits for very long. You may feel like you could never be the kind of sensible man described above, at least on a consistent basis. If so, take heart and have hope. David was commended as a man after God's own heart (1 Samuel 13:14) even though he was far from perfect in his behavior, "for God sees not as man sees, for man looks at the outward appearance, but Yahweh looks at the heart" (1 Samuel 16:7). And even after some of his greatest sins, God still used David to write profound and powerful Psalms that have blessed God's people for three thousand years. Some of those Psalms were even written because of David's sin (e.g., Psalm 32, 51). Though God hates sin, He is able to turn anything around for good. Even the Apostle Paul, more than twenty years after he became a Christian, called himself a "wretched man" who struggled desperately with sin (Romans 7:14–25). But he took heart and had hope because he knew that "there is now no condemnation for those who are in Christ Jesus" (Romans 8:1). Because of God's grace in Christ, God loves you and can use you just as much on your worst days as your best, and no matter where you are on your spiritual journey, He promises to complete the work He has begun in you (Philippians 1:6).

HOW TO BE SENSIBLE

You should never seek to be more sensible in order to earn the love and favor of God. That has been already accomplished for you in Christ. Instead, out of gratitude to Him, you should want to grow spiritually as a way of pleasing Him and knowing Him more intimately. So practically speaking, what should you do? Remember that all we do for Christ, we do in dependence on the power of the Holy Spirit and in obedience to the Word of God with a willingness to submit to Christ as King over every area of life. What are some specific ways that you can pursue living a sensible lifestyle?

"...the sensible man knows the truth about what needs to be done every hour of each day and carefully considers the best way to do it ahead of time."

BE GOAL-ORIENTED

The sensible man has a game plan for this game called life. Like Nehemiah when he rebuilt the walls of Jerusalem (Nehemiah 2:5–8), the sensible man knows the truth about what needs to be done every hour of each day and carefully considers the best way to do it ahead of time. He does not approach life, especially the spiritual aspects of life, the way that Christopher Columbus stumbled upon North America. He did not know where he was going at first, and when he got there, he did not know where he was, and finally, when he returned to Spain, he did not know where he had been.

In contrast, a sensible man sets goals in each aspect of his life. He sets goals for his heart before the Lord, his time in prayer, his study of Scripture, his church ministry, those who he will evangelize and disciple, those who will mentor him, and his future influence for God's glory. He sets goals concerning his spouse, his children, and his parents, thinking biblically through their needs and what is best for them. He sets goals for his work and career path, his physical strength, his well-being and diet, the development of his mind, the ordering of his finances, and his social relationships. His calendar reflects his priorities. The sensible young man is committed to, and making progress toward, the physical and spiritual goals he sets in his life.

The sensible man knows where he is going. When you aim at nothing, you will hit it every time. So the sensible young man makes goals that are measurable and achievable: "I will spend 30 minutes in the Word and prayer every day," "I will encourage three people today," "I will stay on task at work all week," "I will ask my unbelieving friend to have lunch with me today," "This week, I will call three of the junior high students I disciple," "I will pray about an older woman who might be able to mentor my wife," and so on. The godly young man heeds the counsel of Ephesians 5:15–16: "Therefore look carefully how you walk, not as unwise but as wise, redeeming the time, because the days are evil."

LIVE BIBLICALLY

A sensible man evaluates and determines his goals in light of the character of God as revealed in the Word of God, then depends upon the Holy Spirit to put forth sanctified labor and steady progress towards those goals.

A sensible man knows that time is short and the pursuit of living out God's Word in everyday life is a must. Jesus repeatedly challenged His followers in this regard, saying, "Now why do you call Me, 'Lord, Lord,' and do not do what I say?" (Luke 6:46). Young men need to live according to the light of God's Word in every aspect of life and not wander around in the darkness of this world.

When I worked at a Christian camp, I experienced many starless nights because of overcast weather. As I would walk back to my room on the edge of the conference center, sometimes it was so dark I could not see my own hand in front of my face. As I navigated the narrow asphalt road that later turned into a dirt path, I had to rely on my hearing to keep me on track. On one side of me I could hear the stream but nothing else. If I heard the crunching of grass and twigs under my feet, it meant I was about to run into a tree on one side of the road or fall off a steep thirty-foot decline on the other side! I also had to fend off frightening thoughts of mountain lions or vampire squirrels ready to pounce on me. On those moonless nights it would often take me about forty minutes instead of ten to arrive back at my room. Without a light to guide my path, those nightly treks took considerably more time and were much more nerve-racking than during the daytime.

Those treks on starless nights illustrate any Christian man who tries to walk with Christ, lead his family, or minister spiritually without biblical goals. He is walking down a pitch-black road, anxiously wandering back and forth, and making very slow progress. Biblical goals light the way and give the man of God direction. As Psalm 119:105 says, "[God's] word is a lamp to my feet and a light to my path." This is why Paul called Titus to teach the young men to be sensible.

"Many who call themselves Christians want to know God's will for their future before they commit to following His direction in the present."

God is Sovereign, but we are responsible for stepping out in dependent, sensible obedience. Many who call themselves Christians want to know God's will for their future before they commit to following His direction in the present. They are not willing to follow God's will right now by obeying His Word regardless of the circumstances. True Christians do wrestle with obedience, but they have been given hearts that desire to submit to Jesus Christ and the authority of Scripture. Paul affirms this in Romans 6:17: "But thanks be to God that though you were slaves of sin, you obeyed from the heart that pattern of teaching to which you were given over." True Christians want to obey God's Word, even though they sometimes fail to obey. As Jesus told his disciples, "If anyone is willing to do His will, he will know about the teaching, whether it is of God or I speak from Myself" (John 7:17). Willingness to obey God is a necessary condition for being led by God and is found in every born again heart.

God has promised to direct His children's steps. Psalm 32:8 says: "I will give you insight and teach you in the way which you should go; I will counsel you with My eye upon you." Do you believe God wants what is best for you? Then trust Him, like Proverbs 3:5–6 says: "Trust in Yahweh with all your heart and do not lean on your own understanding. In all your ways acknowledge Him, and He will make your paths straight." God's Word will always direct your path if you are willing to follow it.

If you are walking in obedience to what you know is right from Scripture, but still are not sure about which way to go in a particular decision, seek wisdom from the general principles of God's Word to help you.

SEEK GOD'S WISDOM

Even when the Bible does not speak directly to a choice you are considering, God has given many general principles that can be helpful. For example:

- Will this spiritually benefit me and my family? (Ephesians 4:29)
- Will this assist my witness to others? (Colossians 4:5-6)
- Will this set a good example for others to follow? (1 Corinthians 11:1)
- Do I have the right motives? (Philippians 1:21)
- Is my conscience clear? (Romans 14:23)
- Will this bring glory to God? (1 Corinthians 10:31)

"Never primarily trust in your own ideas and feelings, remembering to never 'lean not on your own understanding' (Proverbs 3:5)."

If you cannot sincerely answer all of those questions with a "yes," then you should reconsider your course of action. If you are still unsure, ask some godly people for their counsel. Never primarily trust in your own ideas and feelings, remembering to never "lean not on your own understanding"(Proverbs 3:5). If godly people who know you well advise you in a different direction, take that input very seriously. Proverbs 15:22 says, "Without consultation, plans are frustrated, but with many counselors they succeed." And Proverbs 11:14 says, "Where there is no guidance the people fall, but in abundance of counselors there is salvation." To be distant from godly Christians who can guide you is foolish, and to be disconnected from a healthy local church will put you at a great disadvantage in your pursuit of godliness. The point bears repeating: one of the biggest needs for young Christian men is to have close relationships with older godly men in the context of a sound local church.

PRACTICE REPENTANCE

A fourth way to live sensibly is to quickly repent of any sin in your life. If you are walking in defiant disobedience in any area, you will need to repent of that sin before you can know God's will in any other aspect of life.

For example, if a young man is fornicating with his girlfriend, neither of them can know whether they should get married until they repent and establish a new pattern of obedience. If a man steals at work, either overtly or by wasting time, he cannot know whether God wants him to ask for a raise. If a Christian student cheats on his exams, he cannot know which school God wants him to attend later. If a young man does not minister with his spiritual gifts in his local church, he will not learn what ministry God wants him to be serving in. Why? When believers commit such sins, they are grieving or quenching the Holy Spirit (Ephesians 4:30, 1 Thessalonians 5:19)—The Holy Spirit is the One who reveals God's will. Unrepentant sin in your life will hinder you from knowing God's will.

Psalm 37:4 says, "Delight yourself in Yahweh; and He will give you the desires of your heart." The secret to living out that verse is to delight yourself in the Lord alone. As you truly delight yourself in Christ alone, the Lord often does change your desire towards His will or reveals His will to you in some manner which then does fulfill the desire of your heart.

Sometimes, the repentance we need is directly related to the way we have been seeking God's will. To be sensible, the single man must listen to the right sources of guidance and make sure he is not listening to the wrong ones. So what voices do you listen to?

Do you listen to your own heart? The Bible says your heart is desperately wicked and can only be fully understood by God (Jeremiah 17:9).

Do you listen to your circumstances? Yes, God can use circumstances, but do you look for "signs" that aren't really there? This mystical approach is like meeting a girl who has the same name as a female heroine from your favorite movie or book series. When you meet "Leia" or "Buttercup" you think it must be a divinely ordained encounter!

Do you listen for "a still small voice" to tell you what to do (audibly or in your mind)? Well, even if you did hear something, how would you know it is God's voice? The voice you think is God's could be your own flesh, a message from the enemy, or just

---

"...the single man must listen to the right sources of guidance and make sure he is not listening to the wrong ones."

---

the result of eating some bad pizza the night before.

I have asked college students at conferences, "If God told you to do one thing and the Bible told you to do another, which would you obey?" This gets them thinking about what the authority should be in their decision-making. To be sensible, the young man must say, "God would never lead me contrary to His Word."

Godly young men will listen first and foremost to the written Word of God—the Bible—because it is God's Word and there is no greater or more reliable authority. In every issue, decision, and problem, train yourself to search the Scriptures for your answers. Then, if the issue remains unclear, humbly ask God for wisdom and others for biblical counsel. The Great Shepherd will always be faithful to feed and lead the sheep who desire to follow Him.

Our mighty Savior lived a sensible life. He demonstrated this, for example, in His masterfully wise responses to those who sought to trick or trap Him. Or even more subtly through the timely decisions to minister in one location before moving on to the next throughout the Gospels. Everything Jesus did manifested great sensibility.

SENSIBILITY AND DATING RELATIONSHIPS

For the young single man and single woman, sensibility gives clarity in the guy-girl, dating, courtship struggle. Growing sensible will give you direction in the midst of today's skewed relationship culture.

Regardless of whether you are dating (where you are responsible for interacting with the opposite sex), or courting (where your parents have a structure for you to follow), most young people find relationships difficult and frustrating. Why are there not more healthy interactions between single Christian men and women? Relationships can be intimidating because born-again Christians have a high view of marriage as a life-long commitment. Christians have rejected the hook-up culture of the world. So when a guy-girl relationship begins to form, there is often a lot of pressure from the Christian community. On your first date, your parents and Christian friends may have you married off before you finish your first round of miniature golf.

"When looking for a life partner, you want to find someone who loves Christ more than she loves you."

The sensible young man, however, has learned that relationships are not based upon appearance but upon character, faithfulness, and reputation. Proverbs 22:1 says, "A good name is to be chosen over great wealth, favor is better than silver and gold." When looking for a life partner, you want to find someone who loves Christ more than she loves you. Look for someone who is proven in ministry (so she will be a good church member), someone who lives by the gospel and shares the gospel (so she understands her purpose on this planet), proven in discipleship (so she will be a good parent), and proven in living out her role as a daughter (so she will be ready to fulfill God's design for a wife).

In a dating or courting relationship, a sensible young man will love selflessly, seek God first, and not deceive or defraud his sister in Christ in any way (Colossians 3:9, 1 Thessalonians 4:6). Don't promise anything until you are ready to promise everything.

"Don't promise anything until you are ready to promise everything."

He doesn't make promises, either with his words or actions, that he's not ready to back up with a proposal. He avoids giving outlandish gifts and spending excessive time with a young lady, falsely communicating a future promise he is not ready to make.

A sensible young man understands that determining God's will for a marriage relationship will take time and cannot be instantaneous. He recognizes the importance of counsel and accountability from others through the process of dating, courtship and engagement.

A sensible man understands that each part of a relationship—spiritual, social, emotional, and physical—needs to develop, all of them growing slowly as you progress from acquaintances to friends, from friends to close friends, from close friends to boyfriend and girlfriend, and further on to engagement and marriage. The romantic and physical aspects of a relationship should lag behind the spiritual. A godly relationship is first built on a foundation of mutual respect and care.

A sensible young man understands that there is a progression of physical expression. Physical contact in a relationship generally progresses from holding hands to appropriate hugging, from hugging to perhaps a light kiss, a light kiss to more serious expressions of affection that only belong in marriage. If a young man is going to keep his way pure before God, then he must determine what expressions are appropriate at each stage of a relationship. It is possible to have some small progression, but not cross the line into lust of the heart or immoral physical intimacy prior to marriage. The young man always remembers that impurity starts in the heart and the mind, and being sensible he knows he must fight the battle in his heart first (Matthew 5:28). He also knows there is some behavior which must be left for marriage as God designed if he is going to please the Lord, not defraud his date, and control his desires (2 Timothy 2:22).

The sensible man will think this all out in advance. He will determine what he will do and will not do, what he will say and will not say, what he will promise and will not promise, what gifts he will give and will not give, where he will go and will not go, so that he will not defraud a woman in a relationship (1 Thessalonians 4:6). To defraud a woman in this context is to take something of hers that does not rightfully belong to you yet, or to take something from her future husband that doesn't belong to you. The sensible young man makes goals and plans that will enable him to keep a clean conscience and be an example to others of how to practice the Bible's teaching about sexual purity (Proverbs 6:32, Song of Songs 8:4, 1 Corinthians 7:1, 1 Timothy 5:2, 1 Thessalonians 4:3–8).

If you want to please God in these ways but are falling short in one or more areas, then first repent of your sin and pursue purity. As you do, remember the good news that "Christ died for our sins...and that He was raised on the third day according to the Scriptures" (1 Corinthians 15:3–4). If you are God's true child, Jesus bore the wrath of God in your place, so now you can experience His love for you, even when you require His discipline for living disobediently (Hebrews 12:10). Our adoption by the Father and union with the Son ensures that we will also partake in His resurrection life by the power of the Holy Spirit. He can empower you to live more sensibly, so ask God to make you more sensible, and work toward that goal by pursuing obedience to God's Word, motivated by gratefulness for God's goodness to you.

FOR PERSONAL REFLECTION & GROUP DISCUSSION:

1. If Paul were writing a letter to young men today, do you think he would put "sensible" first on his list like he did with Titus? Why or why not?

2. What does the phrase "of sound mind" mean when people use it today? How is that similar to or different from what Paul meant by "sensible"?

3. How would you counsel a young man who says to you, "I know I should be more sensible in all the ways discussed in this chapter, but I feel depressed and hopeless because I am so far from what I ought to be"?

4. What is "common sense" and how might it relate to the content of this chapter?

5. What does the Bible say about what kind of person you should marry, and what kind of person you should not pursue?

6

LET THE MEN BE EXAMPLES
THE NECESSITY OF GOOD WORKS

"In all things show yourself to be a model of good works."

TITUS 2:7

To me, most auto racing is an accident waiting to happen. But occasionally I tune in on Memorial Day to find out who will win the Indianapolis 500. If you catch the beginning, you will see the race begin with a beautiful new pace car, specially chosen each year to start in front of the professional NASCAR drivers and lead them around the track for a few laps. The pace car guarantees every driver receives a fair chance by making sure that all the cars are in their proper position and moving at a uniform speed when the green starting flag is dropped. When the race is ready to start, the pace car quickly moves out of the way.

In the race of the Christian life, Jesus Christ calls upon men to set the pace by living a life marked by good works. God commands each of his men to be a model for others to follow.

THE IMPORTANCE OF GOOD WORKS

The Bible teaches that what we do impacts those around us. For instance, Philippians 3:17 says, "Brothers, join in following my example, and look for those who walk according to the pattern you have in us." 2 Thessalonians 3:9 refers to "offer[ing] ourselves as a model for you, so that you would imitate us." In 1 Timothy 4:12 Paul charges Timothy, "Show yourself as a model to those who believe in word, conduct, love, faith and purity." And Paul tells the whole church at Corinth, "Be imitators of me, just as I also am of Christ" (1 Corinthians 11:1). God wants our actions to make an impact for good in others' lives. Real spiritual leadership and true male headship cannot exist without a commitment to setting an example that is worth following.

Being a model of good works is not only about encouraging other Christians. It is also one of the ways we can become a more effective witness to the unsaved with the good news of Jesus Christ. As 1 Peter 2:12 says to Christians, "[Keep] your conduct excellent among the Gentiles, so that in the thing which they slander you as evildoers, they may because of your good works, as they observe them, glorify God in the day of visitation." The "day of visitation" refers to the Day of Judgment when we will stand before Christ and give account for our lives. Peter is encouraging believers by highlighting how wonderful it would be to find out on Judgment Day that God used our lives and testimonies to bring people to faith in Christ. Jesus said something similar in the Sermon on the Mount: "Let your light shine before men in such a way that they may see your good works, and glorify your Father who is in heaven" (Matthew 5:16).

As you live dependent upon the Holy Spirit according to the Word of God, the Lord wants you to exercise your will and choose to demonstrate your faith in the form of good works. This kind of life encourages people to submit to Christ in salvation and glorify God in heaven as God's children. The greatest impact we can have on our world is not rallying people to vote or peacefully protest. Instead, it is pursuing Christ and allowing the Holy Spirit to shine through us with biblically-minded good works at home, school, church, work, and in our neighborhood.

Since God calls all of His children to be doers of good works, it follows that men, who are called to be spiritual leaders, ought to be particularly exemplary in this. To be a God-honoring spiritual head, a truly loving husband, a biblically-minded father, or a godly single man, you will need to be a pacesetter when it comes to good works.

As you engage with the content of this chapter, ask yourself these questions: *What kind of doer of good works am I?* Is my faith lived out through works? Is my love shown in action? Is my commitment to Christ coupled with behavior that flows out of a transformed heart? Do I find myself doing things for others because Christ did everything for me?

"Is my commitment to Christ coupled with behavior that flows out of a transformed heart? Do I find myself doing things for others because Christ did everything for me?"

As men, we need to take these questions a step further. Do we "lead the pack" in terms of the good works we perform? Do we set the pace for other Christians by being the first to serve, the first to give, and the first to think about the needs of others? If the answer to any of those questions is "no," then we are not the kind of men God calls us to be.

MOTIVATIONS FOR GOOD WORKS

As we have already seen, in Titus 2:6–8, Paul is working through a list of essential qualities for godly young men. At the beginning of verse 7, Paul tells Titus, "In all things show yourself to be a model of good works." In the last chapter of this book, we learned that a godly man is sensible, meaning that he is a self-controlled individual who is committed to making biblically minded, Christ-honoring decisions. Now Paul adds to the profile of the godly man by saying that we are to be pacesetters in living out a life of good works. But to become such an example, you first need to understand that, in God's mind, good works are a crucial aspect of what every Christian is called to do. Besides our impact on others, the following are additional reasons why good works are important.

PROOF OF FAITH

Good works are an evidence of true saving faith. James 2:17–20 teaches us that true faith will show itself in believers' lives, particularly by their practice of good works. James says, "Even so faith, if it has no works, is dead by itself. But someone will say, 'You have faith; and I have works. Show me your faith without the works, and I will show you my faith by my works.' You believe that God is one. You do well; the demons also believe, and shudder. But are you willing to recognize, you foolish fellow, that faith without works is useless?"

God, through James, is teaching that if you do not live a life that is marked by good works, you are demonstrating that your faith is dead—which is no faith at all. Dead faith is non-faith! Dead faith is no faith! We must not forget what Martin Luther often said, that "we are saved by faith alone, but the faith that saves is never alone." True faith will always show itself with good works.

Sadly, a common belief in some circles is that a person can be a Christian without producing any fruit or performing any good works. According to this line of reasoning, there can be a Christian who perpetually lives like a non-Christian. The term for this is "carnal Christians," but there is no such thing! The Bible describes only two categories of people—Christians and non-Christians. There is no third category of a Christian who lives like a non-Christian.

What Paul says in 1 Corinthians 6:9–11 eliminates the possibility of such a category:

> *Or do you not know that the unrighteous will not inherit the kingdom of God? Do not be deceived; neither the sexually immoral, nor idolaters, nor adulterers, nor effeminate, nor homosexuals, nor thieves, nor the greedy, nor drunkards, nor revilers, nor swindlers, will inherit the kingdom of God. And such were some of you; but you were washed, but you were sanctified, but you were justified in the name of the Lord Jesus Christ and in the Spirit of our God.*

If people who claim to know Christ are known for their ongoing, unrepentant sinfulness, they can have no true assurance of salvation (2 Corinthians 13:5, 2 Peter 1:5–11). If they are living like the world and loving the world, they cannot legitimately claim to be a Christian (1 John 2:15–17).

Consider Galatians 5:19–21, which says, "Now the deeds of the flesh are evident, which are: sexual immorality, impurity, sensuality, idolatry, sorcery, enmities, strife, jealousy, outbursts of anger, selfish ambition, dissensions, factions, envying, drunkenness, carousing, and things like these, of which I forewarn you, just as I have forewarned you, that those who practice such things will not inherit the kingdom of God." Yes, Christians may stumble on the path of righteousness, and yes, they can fall into the way of the flesh, and yes, they will sin. But a truly regenerate follower of Christ will not remain in those sinful patterns and practices. If you have trusted in Jesus, you are born-again and will have a heart that wants to know, love, and obey Jesus Christ.

Our Lord made this clear in Matthew 7:22–23: "Many will say to Me on that day, 'Lord, Lord, in Your name did we not prophesy, and in Your name cast out demons, and in Your name do many miracles?' And then I will declare to them, 'I never knew you; depart from Me, you who practice lawlessness.'"

OUR PURPOSE AS CHRISTIANS

Good works are an important part of the Christian life. God has planned good works for each of his children, and for every local church. Consider what Paul says in his letter to the church at Ephesus. After explaining how the Ephesian Christians were not saved based on their own merit, but solely because of the grace of God, Paul tells us that before God created us, He pre-planned good works that would be accomplished through us for the benefit of Christ's church. Ephesians 2:10 says, "We are His workmanship, created in Christ Jesus for good works, which God prepared beforehand so that we would walk in them."

> **"God did not just pre-ordain our eternal salvation in heaven, but also the works we would do for Him in this life."**

God did not just pre-ordain our eternal salvation in heaven, but also the works we would do for Him in this life. This verse also shows the fallacy of the kind of thinking that says, "If we believe God planned everything, then we won't have any motivation to do anything ourselves, like prayer or evangelism." No, in fact, it is the opposite—God's gracious sovereign plan actually provides motivation for us to choose and act, because God is working through us and makes our good works possible.

Our loving God is Sovereign and has pre-planned our lives to be filled with good works. That means all born-again believers will do them. So if you have not joyfully embraced this divine purpose for your life, you have either not fully understood it yet or you are not a true Christian. God can accomplish His sovereign will with or without you, but He wants to accomplish it through you. Galatians 2:20 is clear, "I have been crucified with Christ, and it is no longer I who live, but Christ lives in me. And the life which I now live in the flesh I live by faith in the Son of God, who loved me and gave Himself up for me." He is the good God in you who produces good works through you. Thank Him for the privilege of being a part of His kingdom plan and pursue His created purpose for you through faithful ministry and the practice of good deeds.

JUDGMENT DAY

Good works are important because they are how Christians will be judged by Jesus Christ. All believers' sins were judged on the cross of Christ and, as Jesus declared, that work is finished! But believers will still give an answer for their lives to the Lord. Every Christian will one day stand before the judgment seat of Christ where we all will be evaluated on the basis of our deeds. At that appointed time, we will receive rewards on the basis of the good works we do. 2 Corinthians 5:10 describes this judgment of believers when it says, "For we must all appear before the judgment seat of Christ, so that each one may be recompensed for his deeds in the body, according to what he has done, whether good or bad."

In that verse Paul simply says that each one of us will be fully exposed before Christ's judgment. Every motive behind every action will be clearly seen, so that those deeds done while we live in this body will be "recompensed" (or paid back, rewarded)—not actions that you intended to do, but actions you have accomplished, determining whether they are useful or useless.

God wants you to know that you will have your deeds exposed

"God wants you to know that you will have your deeds exposed before the never-failing scrutiny of Christ Himself."

before the never-failing scrutiny of Christ Himself. This judgment is one of reward only (often called the "Bema Seat"). It's the time and place where you will stand before the Judge of all mankind and give account for your life. Christ is determined to reward you for the good works you do in this life, evaluating whether those works were useful or useless (which is the literal meaning of "good" and "bad" from 2 Corinthians 5:10 and 1 Corinthians 3:12–15). All those works that have been done for God's glory and in the power of the Spirit will be deemed useful and rewardable. But all those works or ministry accomplished in your own strength, for your own glory, will be deemed useless and rewardless.

As a believer, all your sins were punished on the cross—past, present, and future sins have been dealt with by God. Yet, when you stand before Christ as a born-again believer at your judgment, it will be your works that He rewards.

The works that are eternal are those done in the power of the Spirit and for the glory of God. But those deeds done by you, when you were not walking in the Spirit, will not be rewarded. If in the process of doing a good deed you were actually functioning in your own flesh's strength, you will not be rewarded for that action. You are still saved, but you lost your reward for that specific action.

Do you serve in ministry in order to feel better about yourself or to be noticed by others? When you do a good deed without the proper motivation of glorifying God, those works will not be rewarded. When your heart's motivation is driven by selfishness or pride, those actions will burn—they are useless, unacceptable, and rewardless. You are still saved, but your actions cannot be categorized as good works. As 2 John 8 says, "See to yourselves, that you do not lose what we accomplished, but that you may receive a full reward."

It is fascinating that it will not only be believers whose deeds are judged, but unbelievers will also have their works reviewed by God before He casts them into hell. Notice how Revelation 20:11–15 tells us that the unsaved will be condemned forever on the basis of their deeds:

> *Then I saw a great white throne and Him who sits upon it, from whose presence earth and heaven fled away, and no place was found for them. Then I saw the dead, the great and the small, standing before the throne, and books were opened; and another book was opened, which is the book of life. And the dead were judged from the things which were written in the books, according to their deeds. And the sea gave up the dead which were in it, and death and Hades gave up the dead which were in them, and they were judged, every one of them according to their deeds. Then death and Hades were thrown into the lake of fire. This is the second death, the lake of fire. And if anyone's name was not found written in the book of life, he was thrown into the lake of fire.*

As you can see, God's judgments are made on the basis of works. A non-Christian can do "good works" in this life—they can be generous, or kind, or even appear gracious, but none of those actions are ultimately acceptable to God, since they were all accomplished in the flesh for their own glory and not in the Spirit for His glory. Born-again believers, on the other hand, will always have some good works in their lives that are done for the glory of God and in the power of the Spirit, and those deeds will be rewarded.

MOTIVE AND POWER

Since only good works done for the glory of God and in the power of the Spirit are acceptable to God and worthy of His reward, a "good work" is not ultimately good because of what you do—it's why and how you do it that makes it good.

> ## "Only God is good, and the only works that can be truly good are those that are done for Him and by Him."

Your motive and source of power are the keys to whether a "good work" is good or not. Only God is good, and the only works that can be truly good are those that are done for Him and by Him. If your motive is to glorify God in the power of the Spirit, then your good deed is acceptable to God. If your motive is to call attention to yourself or you perform the deed in your own strength, even though it might appear great to others, it is not acceptable to God. Your reward for that specific action is lost.

Right after Paul exhorts the Corinthian church to not act in a fleshly manner, he describes what happens at the judgment seat of Christ to the Christian who does good works with wrong motives and serves in his own strength. Paul writes in 1 Corinthians 3:12–15, "Now if anyone builds on the foundation with gold, silver, precious stones, wood, hay, straw, each man's work will become evident, for the day will indicate it because it is revealed with fire, and the fire itself will test the quality of each man's work. If any man's work which he has built on it remains, he will receive a reward. If any man's work is burned up, he will suffer loss, but he himself will be saved, yet so as through fire."

Just before Paul wrote the letter to the Corinthians, a fire had ravaged the city of Corinth. The only buildings that stood were the ones made of marble, but all the wood and straw buildings burned to the ground and nothing remained. Drawing upon that event, Paul describes a man who has accumulated a lot of good works, but they do not stand the scrutiny of divine evaluation (the "fire"). His deeds were not done for God's glory and they were not accomplished in God's strength, therefore they were not acceptable to the Lord. They did not count. They were not rewardable. So he will "suffer loss" at the judgment, but he will still be saved.

As a Christian man, your motives in ministry are so important to God. In Acts 4:32–37, from the early history of the Christian church, we see an example of a good deed done with the right motives when Barnabas sold some land and gave the proceeds of the sale to the church:

> And the congregation of those who believed were of one heart and soul, and not one was saying that any of his possessions was his own, but, for them, everything was common.... For there was not a needy person among them, for all who were owners of land or houses would sell them and bring the proceeds of the sales and lay them at the apostles' feet, and they would be distributed to each as any had need. Now Joseph, a Levite of Cyprian birth, who was also called Barnabas by the apostles (which translated means Son of Encouragement), and who owned a field, sold it and brought the money and laid it at the apostles' feet.

Barnabas had a right heart and his good deed honored God. In Acts 5:1–5, however, we see a similar act of giving, but this time with the wrong motives. Wanting to look good, a man named Ananias said that he gave all the money he had pledged, but in fact, he lied. Scripture tells the story:

> *A man named Ananias, with his wife Sapphira, sold a piece of property, and kept back some of the price for himself, with his wife's full knowledge. And bringing a portion of it, he laid it at the apostles' feet. But Peter said, "Ananias, why has Satan filled your heart to lie to the Holy Spirit and to keep back some of the price of the land? While it remained unsold, did it not remain your own? And after it was sold, was it not under your authority? Why is it that you laid this deed in your heart? You have not lied to men but to God." And as he heard these words, Ananias fell down and breathed his last; and great fear came over all who heard.*

Many truths can be learned from this passage, and one of them concerns the motive for good works. Between Barnabas and Ananias (and his wife Sapphira, who was also struck dead), the motive made all the difference.

The importance of performing good works is stressed throughout the book of Titus (e.g., Titus 2:14, 3:1, 3:8). Good works that godly young men perform are an evidence of true faith and are what we are created for. And good works will be a criterion for judgment when we stand before Christ and receive eternal rewards for those that were performed for God's glory.

A CLOSER LOOK AT THE COMMAND

Good works are not only an important part of every Christian's life in service to Christ—they are an essential requirement for spiritual leadership. When Paul says, "In all things show yourself to be a model of good works" (Titus 2:7), he addresses Titus directly. Paul tells Titus this specifically in light of the younger man's ministry of establishing churches on Crete. We will consider some implications of this command for young men today, especially those who want to be used by God in ministering to others.

FOCUS ON GOOD WORKS

When Paul wrote "show yourself," he did so in an emphatic manner. In the Greek, the sentence reads like this: "yourself showing a model of good works." It is as if Paul wants to make sure Titus gets the message, and the Holy Spirit wants to remind us how important this is. You—young man Titus, and you—young men, do this! Also, the word translated "show" is a present participle ("showing"), as good works are to be a continual preoccupation and a ready resource for the godly man. They are not just to be done on random occasions but should be a part of every aspect of your life. The godly young man should be known for his honorable actions.

"...good works are to be a continual preoccupation and a ready resource for the godly man."

The word Paul uses for "show" here also has a unique meaning that will help us to understand why good works are important. It is built from two different Greek words that, when put together, give it a special emphasis.

The first word making up the Greek word for "show" in Titus 2:7 means "to provide, grant, furnish, or supply." It is the same word used in Acts 16:16, where a certain slave girl is described as "bringing [or supplying] her masters much profit by fortune-telling." It is the same word used in Acts 19:24 to describe Demetrius the silversmith, who was "bringing no little business to the craftsmen." The Greek word is used again in 1 Timothy 6:17 where it is translated "supplies": "Command those who are rich in this present age not to be haughty or to set their hope on the uncertainty of riches, but on God, who richly supplies us with all things to enjoy." Considering these various cross-references, the word "show" in Titus 2:7 carries with it the idea of being a selfless well of endless resources.

The second word making up the Greek word for "show" means "to turn one's mind towards, to pay attention, or to be concerned about or occupied with." This was what Paul did not want Timothy to do when he said not to "pay attention to myths and endless genealogies, which give rise to mere speculation rather than furthering the stewardship from God which is by faith" (1 Timothy 1:4). The word is again used to describe what Paul did want Timothy to do in 1 Timothy 4:13—"give attention to the public reading of Scripture, to exhortation and teaching." Paul says that Timothy should not occupy himself with false teaching because of where it leads, but that he should focus on the public reading and proclamation of Scripture.

Paul puts those two words together in the word translated "show," so he is commanding Titus and godly men of every generation to be preoccupied with how to show good works. The godly young man should ask himself each day, *What good deed can I do?*

Every word in Titus 2:7 is loaded with the idea that God fervently desires young men to seek out opportunities to do good works. Even the words for "good" and "works" tell the same story. The word for "good" means that which is suitable and useful; in other words, not an empty promise, but an action that actually makes a difference in people's lives. And the word for "works" could also be translated "tasks" or "employment." This is the Christian man's job— not from nine-to-five, but twenty-four hours a day,

"This is the Christian man's job— not from nine-to-five, but twenty-four hours a day, continually living out a good-deed mindset."

continually living out a good-deed mindset. Living this way is not merely an outward duty or a church function for others to watch, but an inner heart quality that overflows in service for others at every opportunity, for God's glory and in the power of the Spirit.

BE AN EXAMPLE FOR OTHERS

When Paul speaks of being a "model" in Titus 2:7, he uses the Greek word tupos, from which we get our English word "type." In the first century, this was the word for a "die"—an image carved out of stone or metal that was used to make an impression upon a coin or to seal a document. Like a die or a cast, our good works are to be a pattern for others to follow. This is the same idea Paul conveys in Philippians 3:17: "Brothers, join in following my example, and look for those who walk according to the pattern you have in us." Godly men should be those who live in a way that other people will want to follow—the kind of person others want to be like.

However, being a "type" is more than being an example. It also means to leave a mark or to make an imprint. This nuance is found in John 20:25, where Thomas is described as being a doubter: "The other disciples were saying to him, 'We have seen the Lord!' But he said to them, 'Unless I see in His hands the imprint of the nails, and put my finger into the place of the nails, and put my hand into His side, I will not believe.'" The word for "imprint" here is tupos—"type." To be a "type" means you must make an impression through your example. You leave a mark that remains on someone's life. Your good works impact others significantly for the glory of God.

This can happen not only as a result of the bigger things we do but also through the little things. Once I was standing and talking with some of my pastoral interns at the beginning of a church family beach day. One of the interns looked behind me and without a word, bolted out of his place and jetted away from us. Turning around, we all saw him run over to a young mother from our church who had just lost her husband. He helped her by lugging all the beach gear while she corralled her four young children. He made an impression on all of us with his example of doing good works.

IMPACT AND INFLUENCE

Let's consider further the results of biblically-motivated and Spirit-produced good works. How influential are the good works a young godly man performs? What kind of impact will they have?

> ### "...good works will affect the way a man leads."

LEADERSHIP

To state it again for emphasis: good works will affect the way a man leads. In fact, a young man's leadership ability is directly linked to his example of good deeds. 1 Peter 5:2 contains the following exhortation to the elders of a church: "Shepherd the flock of God among you, overseeing not under compulsion, but willingly, according to God; and not for dishonest gain, but with eagerness." Then, in the next verse, Peter says, "Nor yet as lording it over those allotted to you, but being examples to the flock." The word "examples" is, again, tupos—meaning "type" or "pattern." As leaders, all men are to establish a pattern in some way. You are to be an example to your family, to your friends, to your fellow workers, to your disciples, and to the fellow believers in your church.

There are two ways to get sheep from one point to another. You can lead them or drive them. In Middle Eastern cultures, the shepherd typically leads the sheep. It is only the butcher who drives them. True leadership does not drive, force, or manipulate. Instead, true spiritual leadership leads by pattern. So for a man to lead, he must be an example of good works. We impact others by Spirit-filled instruction from God's Word and Spirit-filled modeling.

CREDIBILITY

Not only will good works impact how a man leads, but they also will give him credibility. He will have a good reputation, which 1 Timothy 3:7 says is a requirement for leaders in the church. Mark 14:6–9 gives us a picture of a heart devoted to a lifestyle of performing good works. After anointing Jesus with expensive perfume worth 300 days' wages, Mary was criticized for her extravagance. But, Jesus said, "Let her alone; why do you bother her? She did a good work to Me. For you always have the poor with you, and whenever you wish you can do good to them; but you do not always have Me. She has done what she could; she anointed My body beforehand for the burial. And truly I say to you, wherever the gospel is proclaimed in the whole world, what this woman did will also be spoken of in memory of her."

In this account, we see the positive power a good deed can have on our reputation. A good deed is a fragrant memory and a lasting impression for the cause of Christ.

Is that what you are known for? If not, what is your reputation? If you are not known first for being a servant, and next for being an example of good works, a very essential element of your Christian character is missing.

WITNESS

Good works provide an effective witness to the lost. A Christian man's commitment to living out good works is going to give him credibility with the unsaved. God's design for the saints is to bring God glory by putting Christ on display to those who don't know Him yet. 1 Peter 2:12 says, "[Keep] your conduct excellent among the Gentiles, so that in the thing which they slander you as evildoers, they may because of your good works, as they observe them, glorify God in the day of visitation."

Note that the Christian's good works are to be observable. Why? So that as the unsaved observe those good works, they are able to see the nature of God Himself. By living out good works, a godly young man is sowing seeds that may later sprout into a response to the gospel. Unbelievers may wonder about the source of those good works, which is God working through the believer. The life of the young man who longs to be a fragrant aroma to God (Ephesians 5:2) will have a powerful impact upon those without Christ.

HOW TO BECOME A MODEL OF GOOD WORKS

If you are not already marked as one who is committed to doing good works, how do you become such a person?

Your main goal should be to keep your eyes fixed on Jesus Christ—the ultimate good-deed-doer. From dining with the hated tax-gatherer Zacchaeus to touching a leper and weeping over Lazarus, our Lord always manifested good works.

You should also recognize that becoming an example of good works starts with doing the little things. As St. Francis de Sales said, "Great occasions for serving God seldom come, but little ones surround us daily." Don't wait for the great tasks. Do the

---

" 'Great occasions for serving God seldom come, but little ones surround us daily.' "

---

little tasks in a great way. Remember the words of Jesus: "You were faithful in a few things; I will put you in charge of many things" (my paraphrase of Luke 19:17). A genuine doer of good works will become faithful in the seemingly insignificant tasks and opportunities that exist all around him every day.

If you cannot do great deeds, commit to faithfully doing little deeds. Let God take care of bringing great things along while you do the little things in a great way every day.

Finally, being an exemplary doer of good works starts with a willingness to be humble. Like Jesus, the Son of God, who washed His disciples' feet, men who will do great things for God are those who do the unseen jobs. They are content to love God in their deeds when no one notices. Humility is an attitude of dying to self and seeking to honor Christ in everything, while taking on the role of a slave in actively serving others. It is to be so pervasive in our lives that 1 Peter 5:5 says we are to be clothed in humility. Those who are humble will seek to obey the Scriptures. They seek to obey the Scripture's commands about serving others regularly and faithfully in ministry within the local church, and they seek to be a witness to the lost by good works and sharing the message of the gospel. They do this not to "get ahead" or to be noticed, but because it is God's will found in God's Word. Their commitment to a life filled with good works will make an incredible impact in this world for God's glory.

FOR PERSONAL REFLECTION & GROUP DISCUSSION:

1. How have you seen the good works of a person influence other Christians or unbelievers in a positive way?

2. What would you say to someone who doesn't live for Christ in any way but believes he is saved because he prayed "the sinner's prayer" as a child? Reference specific Scriptures.

3. What are some ways you can cultivate good works in the "little things" of your life, and how do you practically plan to do that?

4. Read 1 Timothy 3:1–13 and Titus 1:5–9. Why do you think Paul lists those requirements for church leadership, and how well do you think they are followed in churches today?

5. Take some time to pray about the "little things" you identified above and the qualifications in 1 Timothy and Titus. Ask God to make you into a model for others, especially in specific areas where you need to grow.

7

LET THE MEN BE DISCERNING
THE LENS OF PURE DOCTRINE

"With purity in doctrine."
TITUS 2:7

What is a real man? How much of our view comes from the culture? Does a man's ability to bench-press 200 pounds, run a mile in under five minutes, maintain 7% body fat, throw a baseball from center field to home plate make him a real man? Does he need to maintain a Civil War-era beard and perform heroic deeds like David's band of fearsome warriors? Are real men those who manage a diverse financial portfolio and drive an expensive European automobile?

As Christians, we do not have to ponder such surface-level questions. Instead, we can consult God's Word. Titus 2:6–8 says, "Likewise urge the younger men to be sensible; in all things show yourself to be a model of good works, with purity in doctrine, dignified, sound in word which is irreproachable, so that the opponent will be put to shame, having nothing bad to say about us."

Remember that Paul was writing to his apostolic assistant and missionary church planter Titus, and also to future generations of Christian believers. It is important to note that his audience is those who are believing Christians. The only way any man can live out the qualities listed in these passages is first to come to saving faith in Jesus Christ and then to follow God's Word, depending exclusively upon the empowering Holy Spirit.

WHY PURSUE THESE QUALITIES AND NOT OTHERS?

Some young men might ask, "Why should I strive to live out these character qualities, or put forth so much effort in pursuing God's design for men?" The book of Titus answers this question.

The first motivation for living out these qualities is knowing what God has accomplished on our behalf through Christ. Titus 2:11–12 says, "For the grace of God has appeared, bringing salvation to all men, instructing us that, denying ungodliness and worldly desires, we should live sensibly, righteously and godly in the present age." All of what Jesus did for us—which we never could have done for ourselves—should motivate all men to live like Him and for Him. When we consider what Jesus Christ has done (and is doing) for us, living in a way that pleases Him by developing the characteristics described in Titus 2:6–8 is a natural response to His amazing grace.

"When believing men are committed to living the way Titus 2:6–8 describes, they will become impactful witnesses for Jesus Christ."

A second motivation for young men to pursue these godly qualities in Titus 2 is to lead others to the Lord. When believing men are committed to living the way Titus 2:6–8 describes, they will become impactful witnesses for Jesus Christ. Their unsaved friends, neighbors, fellow workers, and classmates will notice their commitment to living out these truths by the power of the Holy Spirit. This evangelistic motive for godliness is found in multiple places in Titus. For instance, according to Titus 2:5, younger women are to strive to be "sensible, pure, workers at home, kind, being subject to their own husbands." Why? "So that the word of God will not be slandered." In Titus 2:8, young men are told to be "sound in word which is irreproachable." Why? "So that the opponent will be put to shame, having nothing bad to say about us." In Titus 2:10, bond-slaves are told they are "not [to be] pilfering, but demonstrating all good faith." Why? "So that they will adorn the doctrine of God our Savior in everything."

When young godly men boldly, aggressively, and dependently pursue the life they are called to here in Titus 2, they will stand out. They will be a light in the darkness of this world for God's glory—winsome to those who don't know Christ, as well as examples to those who do know Him.

If God's grace has gripped your heart, if you desire to become an effective witness for Christ and you long to bring God glory by the way you live, the qualities Paul mentions in Titus 2:6–8 are qualities to pursue with all your heart. One of the most important qualities of a godly man is to be pure in doctrine. Unfortunately, most believers tend to think this quality is reserved for seminary students and pastors. But God's Word calls all young men to be pure in doctrine.

WHAT DOES IT MEAN TO BE PURE IN DOCTRINE?

Previous chapters in this book have highlighted several key characteristics for the godly man to pursue. Being pure in doctrine is also critical for the godly young man. In God's eyes, you don't need to be able to military press 300 pounds, but you do need to be pure in doctrine.

If you try to drive a car with a timing belt that's failing, you will notice that the car will chug, cough, or stop altogether. Cars with belt problems will run slow and lack power, and they may not even start in the first place. Pure doctrine is like a good timing belt—it keeps a man's spiritual life running smoothly and effectively. Those men who live by the timeless truths given to us in the Bible have God's guidance, wisdom, strength, and resources to empower and sustain them. If, on the other hand, the principles a man lives by are wrong, mixed, or diluted, his spiritual timing will be off. He will lack direction and power, and will not be able to make good use of the resources God has made available to him.

When a man rejoices in truth that he likes but rejects biblical truth that he doesn't like, he is not pure in doctrine. When a man mixes human reasoning and his own opinions with Scripture, he is not pure in doctrine. When a man rarely reads, studies, or applies the Word of God, he is not pure in doctrine. When a man thinks spiritual maturity will happen automatically simply because he attends a Bible-teaching church, he is not pure in doctrine. When a man treats public worship, ministry, or sacrificial giving as optional, he is not pure in doctrine. When a man expresses unrighteous anger verbally and refuses to apologize and seek forgiveness, he is not pure in doctrine. When a man says he hates adultery, fornication, and other deadly sins, but watches those same sins in entertainment or pornography, he is not pure in doctrine. When comfort and convenience are the main goals of a man's life, while he rarely puts forth any effort in his relationship with God, he is not pure in doctrine.

Those who are not pure in doctrine live by their own notions of what the Bible teaches, function by self-designed rules, or follow tradition more than truth. Such a man does not interpret the Word correctly, learn it diligently, or apply it wisely. His sword skills are rusty and he is not ready to witness, make godly decisions, lead his family, or otherwise live by the truth.

By contrast, a man who is pure in doctrine learns biblical truth and applies it by the power of the Spirit to his life. He is constantly honing his ability to wield the sword of the Spirit so he is skillful when he implements this spiritual weapon. When a door opens to share the gospel with the lost, he is ready. When a moral dilemma faces him at work, he is ready. When opportunities arise to lead his family in the truth, he is ready. When he enters into a relationship with a young woman, he is ready to conduct himself in a wise and holy manner. He lives according to the Bible, depending on and following God's truth.

How skilled are you at wielding the sword? Are you pursuing doctrinal purity? This is in keeping with what God predicted would happen: "For the time will come when they will not endure sound doctrine; but wanting to have their ears tickled, they will accumulate for themselves teachers in accordance to their own desires" (2 Timothy 4:3). Even today, there are many who are "peddling the word of God" (2 Corinthians 2:17) as they seek to grow churches as though they were businesses. There are many who attempt to make people feel good by twisting the Scriptures. These are crafty people who are "adulterating the word of God" (2 Corinthians 4:2) in order to satisfy their own lusts.

"...a man who is pure in doctrine... is constantly honing his ability to wield the sword of the Spirit so he is skillful when he implements this spiritual weapon."

HOW CAN YOU BE PURE IN DOCTRINE?

With the vast majority of today's churches being in such dire straits, how can a young man become—and remain—biblically sharp? How can young men grow to be "pure in doctrine"?

PURSUE TRUTH

First, the godly young man will be committed to passionately pursuing untainted truth. When Paul charges Titus to be pure in his doctrine, the Greek word he uses for "pure" literally means "no corruption," "no spoiling," "no destroying," or "no leading astray."

When you mix white paint with another color, the paint is no longer white. When you accidentally splash bleach on your favorite blue shirt, the shirt is no longer completely blue. When you add water to gasoline, its power is diluted, and the chances of doing damage to a motor increases. It is the same with biblical truth. Biblical truth is to remain unmixed. When you add human wisdom, secular business ideas, or psychological concepts to biblical truth, you destroy its purity, power, effectiveness, and clarity. It is no longer God's Word, but a distorted word. It is not living and active, but dead and lifeless. Thus, to be "pure in doctrine" is to keep truth untainted so it does not become partial truth (at best) or mere human wisdom (at worst).

The godly young man understands that correctly interpreting the Bible is the path to pure doctrine. Such accurate interpretation only results from determining the author's intended meaning of any verse in Scripture. And the author's intended meaning is determined by correct hermeneutics. That means the only right understanding of a passage is based upon a literal reading that honors context, original language, culture, and geography. Practically, you apply the principles of hermeneutics by asking questions like, "What did Paul mean when he wrote Titus around 2,000 years ago while Titus was ministering on Crete as Paul's apostolic representative?" Determining the answer to that question will yield the correct interpretation, leading to pure doctrine.

The need for men to be pure in doctrine is found throughout the New Testament. God does not want us messing up His Word. For instance, the Lord Jesus Christ, in Matthew 15:8–9, warns us even today when He says, "This people honors Me with their lips, but their heart is far away from Me. But in vain do they worship Me, teaching as doctrines the commands of men." The Lord is telling His followers not to embrace teaching that is made up of human ideas. Instead, we are to be committed to biblical principles above all else. Likewise, Paul warned Titus and all future ministers of the gospel that they should not be "paying attention to... commandments of men who turn away from the truth" (Titus 1:14). The author of Psalm 119:140 says, "Your word is exceedingly refined." Finally, Peter charged followers of Christ, "Like newborn babies, long for the pure milk of the word" (1 Peter 2:2).

The Bible is to remain pure, unmixed, and untainted. When we read the Bible, study the Bible, and teach the Bible, we are to be like waiters. Our job is to deliver God's Word to the table of hungry hearts without altering it or messing it up in any way.

Biblically-guided men do not forget that 90% truth mixed with 10% lie is all lie. Just like a pharmacist who misinterprets the instructions for a medicine and accidentally adds a poison to it, the same kind of corruption happens to Scripture when it is misinterpreted and made to say something other than what God originally intended.

"Scripture will be their compass, their filter, their food, their treasure, and the lens through which they see all of life."

Young men who desire to be pure in doctrine will be biblically guided men. Scripture will be their compass, their filter, their food, their treasure, and the lens through which they see all of life. They will evaluate every speaker, every event, every church, every relationship and every new wind of doctrine by the trustworthy Word of God. They will work at keeping the truth unspoiled, untainted, and uncorrupted.

Biblically-guided men believe it is better to be divided because of truth than to be united in error. They believe it is better to speak truth that hurts (but eventually heals) than to speak falsehood that comforts (but poisons). Because of their commitment to Scripture, they understand that it is better to be hated for telling the truth than to be loved for telling a lie, even if they stand alone or are part of a small minority. Godly young men desire to be men of 'no compromise' like Daniel and his three friends, rather than their other youthful companions who ended up compromising God's Word (the Law) on their diet (Daniel 1:8-16).

SEEK INSTRUCTION

When a young man is committed to pure doctrine, he will constantly be seeking out, receiving, and relying upon healthy biblical teaching. The Greek word for "doctrine" (didaskalia) in Titus 2:7 means "instruction." What a young man listens to, reads, meditates on, and talks about in conversation will dramatically affect his purity of doctrine. This is why doctrine should be

> **"What a young man listens to, reads, meditates on, and talks about in conversation will dramatically affect his purity of doctrine."**

considered the Christian man's foundation, food, and fight. Other passages in the New Testament point to these three truths.

To say that pure doctrine is the godly young man's **foundation** is to echo what Paul teaches in Ephesians 4:14–15: "We are no longer to be children, tossed here and there by waves and carried about by every wind of doctrine, by the trickery of men, by craftiness in deceitful scheming, but speaking the truth in love, we are to grow up in all aspects into Him who is the head, that is Christ." As men, we are not to be swayed by every new idea or approach because we have a foundation of truth to stand upon. Like a huge rock in a stormy sea, sound doctrine is steady and unmovable. Our foundation of biblical truth is certain and unwavering. So the godly young man is not looking for new ideas but old revealed truth. You want to know what the apostles taught, not what some opinionated blogger thinks.

When speaking to the lost about their future destiny, the godly young man will confidently express how to lay claim to eternity in heaven with Christ and to avoid eternal torment in hell. The young man doesn't dance around difficult aspects of biblical theology but states the truth as God revealed it through His chosen prophets and apostles.

As men who are either fathers or future fathers, we must be committed to obeying the commands in Ephesians 6:4, which are directed at dads: "Fathers, do not provoke your children to anger; but bring them up in the discipline and instruction of the Lord." That verse (along with the only other one in the New Testament directly about parenting, Colossians 3:21) tells fathers to use the tools of faithful discipline and doctrinal instruction to raise up children to follow Christ. God did not give that assignment to mothers, but to fathers. Paul specifically uses the words "parents" and "mother" in Ephesians 6:1–2, so if he wanted to include mothers in verse 4, he would have. But he did not. He placed the responsibility of parental discipleship squarely on the shoulders of men.

A godly father knows it is his job to learn the truth, know the truth, and live the truth. He is to model and instruct his children in it. He understands he is not perfect, but makes a life-long commitment to mature in his faith. As his faith grows deeper, so does his love for God, his wife, and children.

The young godly man knows he must embrace sound doctrine so that he can fulfill that God-given assignment in the future. All godly men recognize that they will one day give an account to the Lord for how they taught and modeled a biblical foundation in the lives of their children.

"A steady diet of junk food will eventually hurt a person physically. A steady diet of bad doctrine will do the same to a person's spiritual life."

To say that pure doctrine is your **food** is to recognize you should constantly be "nourished on the words of the faith and of the sound doctrine which you have been following" (1 Timothy 4:6). The young godly man heeds the warning of 1 Timothy 4:1: "In later times some will fall away from the faith, paying attention to deceitful spirits and doctrines of demons." If we fed our children nothing but junk food, eventually they would become weak, sick, or worse. A steady diet of junk food will eventually hurt a person physically. A steady diet of bad doctrine will do the same to a person's spiritual life. God has designed us so that our spiritual diet not merely be milk but meat, so that we can grow spiritually strong (1 Corinthians 3:2). Constantly feeding on empty calories— spiritually speaking—will hamper and harm our walk with God.

Pure doctrine is also the young godly man's **fight**. This is seen in Paul's instruction to Titus for elders on Crete in Titus 1:9, where he says that each church leader is to be "holding fast the faithful word which is in accordance with the teaching, that he will be able both to exhort in sound doctrine and to reprove those who contradict." Young men who want to be pure in doctrine need to be able to correct those who promote error and warn others about that which is contrary to sound teaching. God wants young men to be pure in doctrine, which means they must fight impure doctrine. Godly men are to know and live out the truth that the Word of God is the "sword of the Spirit" (Ephesians 6:17), which we use to fight spiritual battles against the evil one (1 John 2:14). The man who is steeped in Scripture and sound doctrine will not be overwhelmed by claims made by cults, false teachers, misguided bloggers, errant authors, and other contentious people. Instead, he will be able to confidently and boldly stand for the truth. Young men need to be discerning as to when to stand for truth and who to confront. Sometimes young men tear into God's sheep over some perceived doctrinal error, when patience, love and grace should be the motivation of their equipping and correction. But there is a need for young men to stand firm and do battle over truth.

COMMITTING TO DISCERNMENT

So how strong are you doctrinally? Are you able to defend your faith? Are you able to uphold the fact that the Bible is the Word of God? Are you able to stand up for the truth that the church is to gather together weekly on Sunday for worship? Are you able to demonstrate biblically that Jesus is the one true God to a Jehovah's Witness? Are you able to show from Scripture that a true Christian will desire to follow Christ as Lord? Are you able to biblically prove that sexual abstinence is God's plan for singles and adultery in marriage is a sin? Are you able to make the biblical case for abortion being murder, homosexuality being a sin, and that those whose lives are characterized by lying or gossiping have no assurance of salvation? In other words, how capable are you in handling the biblical sword?

Are you willing to grow in biblical discernment as a good soldier of the Lord Jesus Christ? If so, here are five commitments you must make in order to sharpen your skills in Scripture.

ACCURATE INTERPRETATION

First, you will need to commit to becoming—and remaining—a correct interpreter of the Word. 2 Timothy 2:15 says, "Be diligent to present yourself approved to God as a workman who does not need to be ashamed, accurately handling the word of truth." When a young man hears, reads, studies, or discusses God's Word, he is to be zealous about interpreting the Word accurately by intently studying its background and context, as well as how each passage fits into the entire doctrinal framework of the Scriptures. A godly man does not play fast and loose with the Bible but instead seeks to discover the author's single intended meaning in any given passage. With the New Testament, men are to ask in their studies, "Is this what the apostle meant to say to the original audience, in its context, in the Greek language, in that culture, 2000 years ago, when he wrote it?" Godly men will work hard to determine accurate interpretation.

A GODLY LIFE

Second, to grow in discernment you will need to commit to living in a way that is consistently aligned with the truth you learn from Scripture. Godly young men do not habitually live contrary to sound teaching. They are not influenced by "sexually immoral persons, homosexuals, kidnappers, liars, perjurers, and whatever else is contrary to sound teaching" (1 Timothy 1:10). Instead, young men who are committed to purity of doctrine will live out the truth of God's Word as a pattern of their lives, heeding the words of Jesus in Luke 11:28: "Blessed are those who hear the word of God and keep it." Such a man is committed to telling the truth even when it takes humility and courage to share it with his parents or girlfriend. By his own convictions he puts in a full day's work at his job, even when no one is watching. He will correct a cashier's mistake by returning money not owed to him. Throughout each day and in many ways, this godly young man models Christlikeness.

"Can you imagine having such an insatiable hunger for God's truth that you would rather study the Bible than enjoy a good meal?"

HUNGER FOR TRUTH

Third, young men should echo the words of Job: "I have not departed from the command of His lips; I have treasured the words of His mouth more than my portion of food" (Job 23:12). Can you imagine having such an insatiable hunger for God's truth that you would rather study the Bible than enjoy a good meal? Have you ever skipped a meal because you were busy learning the Word?

Do you remember how hard you worked to get an "A" in school? A man who is committed to purity in his doctrine will strive to get an "A" in his study of God's Word and theology. He meditates, memorizes, researches, takes notes, attends classes and fosters discussion—all to grow in his understanding of God's Word. Jesus said in Matthew 5:6, "Blessed are those who hunger and thirst for righteousness, for they shall be satisfied." The biblically-guided man experiences great satisfaction when his thirst for truth is quenched in the fountain of God's Word.

"So make your stand on biblical theology and let it have authority over your thinking, your emotions, and your experiences."

BIBLICAL AUTHORITY

Fourth, you will need to make your decisions based upon the Bible. The biblically-guided man lives by the words of Psalm 119:105: "Your word is a lamp to my feet and a light to my path." Does the Bible light your path? Do you allow Scripture to determine what you should and shouldn't do? Does your study of it teach you how to best exalt Christ? Do you allow the Bible to inform you as to how to invest your time, spend your money, what woman to date, or if married, how to love your wife, and from what to avert your eyes? Does God's Word settle your views on current issues? When you open your mouth, do you talk mostly about your opinions, or do you speak about what the Bible teaches?

If you want to grow in discernment, you cannot allow emotions or experiences determine truth. Peter made this clear in 2 Peter 1:19. Just after verses 16–18, which describes the Transfiguration of Christ—a powerful physical and emotional experience that Peter witnessed live—he makes this statement in the very next verse: "We have as more sure the prophetic word, to which you do well to pay attention as to a lamp shining in a dark place, until the day dawns and the morning star arises in your hearts."

What is more certain than Peter's amazing and overwhelming experience on the Mount of Transfiguration? God's Word. Peter says the Bible is more sure, more certain than any spiritual experience we might have, even a true experience. So make your stand on biblical theology and let it have authority over your thinking, your emotions, and your experiences. Learn to judge everything that happens in your life by what the Bible says.

TIME WITH THE LORD

Young men will need to spend time with Christ through His Word if they want to grow in discernment. Like a best friend, the man who is pure in doctrine spends regular time communing with Christ. He looks beyond the printed pages of the Bible and into the face of Christ. He views Scripture not as a wall but as a window to spend time with the One he loves.

> **"...the man who is pure in doctrine spends regular time communing with Christ. He looks beyond the printed pages of the Bible and into the face of Christ."**

Only those who read and study the Scriptures have an intimate relationship with Christ. No relationship can be healthy unless there is time spent communicating. And the Scriptures are the voice of God to the believer. And, speaking of relationships, the only guy-girl relationships that will be blessed by God and pleasing to Him will be those that are determined by and guided by God's Word and sound theology. What you talk about, where you go on a date, and how you progress as a couple must be directed by God's Word.

Becoming a biblically-informed and biblically-centered man of God will not happen instantaneously. It will not happen at a single church service, nor will it happen without you putting forth the mandatory work of reading and studying the Word of God. It will take time and effort to become pure in doctrine. Growing into a mature, biblically-guided man of the Word is a process that begins with a fundamental commitment to developing habits (called spiritual disciplines). With the empowerment of the indwelling Holy Spirit, you can grow in your biblical knowledge and develop essential convictions, which in turn will fuel increasingly godly character and courage for ministry and witness.

"With the empowerment of the indwelling Holy Spirit, you can grow in your biblical knowledge and develop essential convictions..."

Howard Rutledge was an Air Force pilot who was shot down and captured in the Vietnam war. His book, *In the Presence of Mine Enemies* (Fleming Revell 1973), describes his captivity as a prisoner of war. The following excerpt illustrates what we have learned in this chapter:

> *During those longer periods of enforced reflection, it became so much easier to separate the important from the trivial, the worthwhile from the waste. For example, in the past, I usually worked or played hard on Sundays and had no time for church. For years Phyllis [his wife] had encouraged me to join the family at church. She never nagged or scolded—she just kept hoping. But I was too busy, too preoccupied, to spend one or two short hours a week thinking about the*

really important things.
Now the sights and sounds and smells of death were all
around me. My hunger for spiritual food soon outdid
my hunger for a steak. Now I wanted to know about
that part of me that will never die. Now I wanted to
talk about God and Christ and the church. But in the
Hanoi Hilton [the name POWs gave their prison camp]
solitary confinement, there was no pastor, no Sunday-
School teacher, no Bible, no hymnbook, no community
of believers to guide and sustain me. I had completely
neglected the spiritual dimension of my life. It took
prison to show me how empty my life is without God.
(Rutledge and White #34)

With all the freedom you have right now, what steps will you take to be pure in doctrine?

FOR PERSONAL REFLECTION & GROUP DISCUSSION:

1. If you asked people in our culture what traits are most important for a man to have, very few would say "purity in doctrine." Why do you think that is?

2. List some ways that God has been good to you, both spiritually and physically, and how each of them provides motivation for you to diligently pursue growth in Christ.

3. What are some specific ways you can seek instruction and learning in sound doctrine, and what practical steps will you take to do so?

4. Select a few of the doctrinal questions mentioned in the paragraph under the heading "Commitment to Discernment" in this chapter. What would you say in those situations?

5. Why do people often give their experience more authority than Scripture, and how do we keep from falling into that error?

8

LET THE MEN BE DIGNIFIED
THE PATHWAY TO RESPECT

"In all things show yourself to be a model...dignified."
TITUS 2:7

Have you noticed that dignity is on the decline today? Basic manners, honoring authority, being on time, a commitment to excellence, and keeping one's promises are becoming increasingly rare. Yet, dignity is a cherished biblical quality that Jesus wants all of His children to have and pursue. As we continue on with our exploration of the profile of a godly young man, Paul adds to the list of essential character qualities the lost trait of living "dignified" (Titus 2:7).

I currently have joined the ranks of being a grandpa. Two of my grandsons live in Hawaii and for many, the Hawaiian name for grandpa is KUKU. (Grandma is TUTU) Most of my friends say that my grandpa name is fitting. As I have learned to play with kids all over again, I use funny voices, do crazy things with balloons and water, spend a lot of time with Legos, do crazy science experiments, go on long walks, wild bike rides, family friendly hikes, watch cartoon kid shows, run on beaches, throw kids in the water, splash, make funny faces, sing silly songs, and not only teach my grandsons the Scripture, but all kinds of facts and funny life issues. I want them to know me as an older man who LOVES Christ and OBEYS His Word, but also can have FUN. Would you call me dignified? Am I being a dignified model for others to follow? Are fathers (and grandfathers) supposed to be fun or should they be aloof? And for the single man, are you to be socially creative, fun, and happy, or steady, stuffy, and stale?

Unfortunately, many people have a wrong view of what it means to be dignified. For instance, in some Christian circles in Russia, a man's "dignity" is associated with refusing to laugh or smile and always maintaining a serious demeanor. The same definition is employed in certain American churches, where "dignity" is portrayed as being an emotionless zombie who does not experience any highs or lows. If these are not accurate pictures of what it means to be dignified, what is a proper definition of this key quality and spiritual pursuit for all young men?

Before we learn more about the quality of dignity mentioned in Titus 2, take these two brief tests.

"If you are dignified, the following will be patterns in your life: you earn respect, the right to be heard, you are courteous, serious, responsible, noble, and followed as a model."

First, the negative dignity test. See how well this description fits you. If you are dignified then you are not, as a pattern of life: touchy, aloof, shallow, petty, dry, prudish, an arguer, one to bear grudges, or one who is unapproachable.

Now here's the positive dignity test. If you are dignified, the following will be patterns in your life: you earn respect, the right to be heard, you are courteous, serious, responsible, noble, and followed as a model.

The goal is to hit low marks on the negative test and high marks on the positive test. How did you do?

DEFINING DIGNITY

Titus 2:7 tells Christian men that whether they are with other Christians, unbelievers, at school, on a date, with friends, with their wives or children, or in any other situation, God expects them to be dignified. Jesus Christ not only insists that our minds be sensible, that our behavior be marked by good works, that our theology be pure—He also expects our social interactions to be dignified. Remember, Titus 2:2 says that the older men should be dignified—Paul now repeats it here for the younger men. The Spirit of God through the Apostle Paul is making clear that dignity is important for all men, old and young, which is why we will invest an entire chapter trying to unpack its meaning and application for every aspect of our lives. As we piece together a biblical definition of dignity in the following pages, you will have a standard for evaluating your life in the light of Scripture.

If you were to run a search on the word "dignity" in the Legacy Standard Bible, you would find that the word appears two other times in the New Testament, and both are in Paul's first letter to Timothy.

The word is found in 1 Timothy 2:1–2: "I exhort that petitions and prayers, requests and thanksgivings, be made for all men, for kings and all who are in authority, so that we may lead a tranquil and quiet life in all godliness and dignity." This passage connects dignity with a life of godliness, so we can see that the biblical use of the word is not just concerned with how other people view us but is Godward in its focus. The second use is in 1 Timothy 3:4, which says that a church elder must be "leading his own household well, having his children in submission with all dignity." Here dignity is connected with self-control and other behaviors proper for children, so it is safe to say that men who are dignified live out a blend of humility, courtesy, seriousness, and respectfulness.

Additional light on the biblical meaning of dignity can be brought into focus by looking at the occurrences of other Greek words related to the one translated that way in 1 Timothy and Titus. Each of these similar words provides further insight concerning what it means to be a dignified man of God. For instance, Paul instructed the church at Philippi, "Whatever is true, whatever is dignified, whatever is right, whatever is pure, whatever is lovely, whatever is commendable, if there is any excellence and if anything worthy of praise, consider these things" (Philippians 4:8). The Greek word translated "dignified" in that verse has the same root as "dignified" in Titus 2:7, which informs us that the godly young man is committed to pursuing a dignified thought life. He will be a man who thinks humbly, courteously, seriously, and respectfully.

The book of Acts contains several cross-references that help expand our understanding of dignity. Acts 13:43 says, "Now when the meeting of the synagogue had broken up, many of the Jews and of the God-fearing proselytes followed Paul and Barnabas, who, speaking to them, were urging them to continue in the grace of God." The word translated "God-fearing" comes from the same root as the one for "dignified" in Titus 2:7. Next, we see that same term "God-fearing" in Acts 13:50, "The Jews incited the God-fearing women of prominence and the leading men of the city." And then in Acts 16:14 we read, "a woman named Lydia, from the city of Thyatira, a seller of purple fabrics, a worshiper of God, was listening, whose heart the Lord opened to pay attention to the things spoken by Paul." The word "worshiper" in this verse also comes from the same root as "dignified" in Titus 2:7.

> ## "To be dignified is to live life on Earth as if you are living in the presence of God."

Taking all these passages together shows us that a dignified Christian is a "worshipful and devout God-fearer." Those who fear God respect and revere Him in their lifestyle, overall attitude, and everyday words and actions. So notice again that the focus here is Godward. To be dignified is to live life on Earth as if you are living in the presence of God. To be dignified is to live knowing that the God of your salvation is watching you, knowing you, and holding you accountable. We saw in chapter 6 that every detail of your life will be evaluated at the judgment seat of Christ. For the believer, your judgment is for reward, since your sins were judged on the cross. This awareness of our Lord's righteous evaluation for reward produces in our hearts a blend of humility, courtesy, seriousness, and respectfulness.

Biblically, dignity is a quality that distinguishes you as one who is no longer a child but a maturing Christian. No matter his age, a man is dignified when he has learned how to live on earth as a citizen of heaven. Whether a collegian or retiree, the dignified man is dependent upon Christ, filled with the Spirit in every circumstance, and sees things consistently from a biblical and heavenly perspective.

The word "dignified" would be almost impossible to act out in a game of charades. How would you portray a quality that is a blend of humility, courtesy, seriousness, and respectability? But the fact

"No matter his age, a man is dignified when he has learned how to live on earth as a citizen of heaven."

that it is difficult to define precisely makes it even more important to understand and practice. So let's take a look at a few scenarios that might help you to begin thinking about dignity.

> **Scenario #1**: You're watching a football game and the referee has just made an incredibly bad call against your team, which costs them the championship. At that moment, what type of response would you consider to be dignified?

> **Scenario #2**: You're driving home on the freeway after a long hot day with no air conditioning, a random driver cuts you off, and you miss your off-ramp. At that moment, what type of response would you consider to be dignified?

> **Scenario #3**: You come back home after a long day of work. You had to skip lunch and have been craving your favorite left-over pizza. You walk in the door, and your roommate is chomping down on the last bit of crust. At that moment, what type of response would you consider to be dignified?

> **Scenario #4**: You are walking out of class and you see your roommate talking to a girl that you like. Your

roommate knew that you were going to ask her out on a date this Friday, but he beat you to the punch. At that moment, what type of response would you consider to be dignified?

What are the marks of a young man who truly has a dignified mind and heart? He will be respectful, responsible, and a representative of the One he worships, Jesus Christ. And he will demonstrate those qualities in his relationships with others.

MARKS OF DIGNITY

RESPECTFUL

A dignified Christian man is, first of all, reverent and honoring toward God. At the root of the Greek word for "dignified" in Titus 2:7 is the idea of worship. All of the Christian life is an expression of worship. A dignified person does not divide his life up into separate "this is for Jesus" and "this is for me" categories. A godly young man does not compartmentalize. He lives all of life in the presence of the God he fears, and that divine accountability is evident in the way he treats others.

Most people know what a microwave dinner is. It is a frozen meal with several courses divided up into sections to keep them separate from one another. Most of us also know what a chicken pot pie is, where all the mixed veggies commingle with the meat in a tasty gravy. Sadly, many men see their lives as a microwave dinner, all compartmentalized into separate sections. The peas of work, the carrots of recreation, the potatoes of family life, and the meat of our church life are all distinct and separate. And as long as their church life appears good, it does not matter if they are a poor witness at work and indifferent at home, because in their minds, everything is separate. Men sometimes mistakenly think, "As long as I read the Word and pray this morning, then everything else in my life, including road rage, rudeness to a client, stealing from the office, impatience with my children — it's all no big deal." Men compartmentalize their lives, but God does not.

But the reality is, our lives before God are like chicken pot pies. Everything is mixed together and viewed as one offering to Him. If we are not loving our wives, then it does not matter that we look good at church or are doing well at work. Our offering is rotten and the aroma we are sending up to the Lord stinks. Our life, which is a living sacrifice to Christ (Romans 12:1–2), is not a sweet-smelling sacrifice but a putrid one. If only one part is rotten, then the entire offering is rotten. If the peas are bad, the entire chicken pot pie is bad.

A man who is dignified seeks to be obedient in every area of his life and to all of God's commands, not just a pre-selected few. Everything he does is for Christ Himself. All work, play, recreation, entertainment, budgeting, resting—every hour of his day—is for Christ and is an expression of worship for the Savior who sacrificially gave all to him.

Next, a dignified young man is respectful toward other people. In his interactions with others, the dignified man shows respect to all, regardless of class or status. Whether he is conversing with a well-known political leader or the local postman, a great man or a young toddler, he recognizes that all people have been created in the image of God (Genesis 1:26) and are therefore worthy of respect.

The dignified young man follows Jesus' example of gentleness (Matthew 11:29) by performing various social graces like opening doors for women, standing up to shake hands, looking individuals in the eye, giving a greeting to passers-by, thanking others for their contributions, valuing the different spiritual gifts of the saints, and assisting anyone who needs help.

Dignified young men seek to comply with proper etiquette and attempt to dress appropriately. They try not to call attention to themselves but seek to point to Christ, since what they say and do is intended to honor their King. Their Godward focus and the awareness that they are accountable to the Lord in all things transforms their everyday behavior and the way they treat others.

"The dignified man is serious about eternal things. He can laugh at himself, but he does not laugh at God or His Word."

Being a dignified man does not mean that you never laugh, or that you cannot enjoy a good time. Acting dignified does not mean you will be haughty, high class, or that you talk down to people.

As I have already affirmed, one of the best ways to describe the dignified young man is to say that he is a person who does not take himself seriously but takes Christ and His Word very seriously. The dignified man is serious about eternal things. He can laugh at himself, but he does not laugh at God or His Word. He isn't overly serious, but he is convinced there are people going to heaven and more going to hell. This sober reality keeps him mindful of the need to share the gospel and thankful for his own salvation. He does not joke about people going to hell, immorality, vulgarity, or anything that is sinful. He does not laugh at what is tragic or at the expense of others. He loves the things that God loves, hates the things that God hates, and grieves over the things that grieve God.

RESPONSIBLE

Coupled with his respectfulness, the dignified young man is also responsible both to God and others. In his responsibilities to the Lord, he enjoys daily communion with Christ and faithfully gathers regularly in corporate worship. He is also regularly involved in a smaller community of Christians (e.g., a small group, community group or discipleship group). He is committed to a local church and exercising his spiritual giftedness as he regularly serves others in the body of Christ. He is sacrificial in his financial giving to the cause of Christ through the church.

A dignified young man recognizes that, first and foremost, he is accountable to God. He keeps Christ as His first love above every other love (Revelation 2:4). This is so important that, if Christ is not above all in your life, it causes a loss of assurance. Jesus says plainly in Luke 14:26, "If anyone comes to Me, and does not hate his own father and mother and wife and children and brothers and sisters, yes, and even his own life, he cannot be My disciple." The dignified man does not allow any relationship (including his closest earthly relationships) to compete with his relationship with Christ. He pursues Christ as his first love.

"The dignified man does not allow any relationship (including his closest earthly relationships) to compete with his relationship with Christ. He pursues Christ as his first love."

The dignified man lives out a dedicated commitment to Christ. Throughout church history, missionaries have grieved over the deaths of their wives or children. Yet, because of their faithfulness to Christ, they remained in the field and continued to reach the lost. Many elders and pastors put Christ above all without neglecting their wives or children—yet there is no question in their family whom Dad loves most—Jesus. Great marriages blossom when

Christ is the first love. Great laymen in churches model dignity because they love Christ more than anyone.

In addition to being responsible to God, the dignified man seeks to be an example in his everyday life to others. Men of dignity are willing to surrender their rights for the sake of a weaker brother. They come alongside struggling Christians to bear their burdens, serve, pray, sacrifice, and give generously to them for the sake of Christ. They do not live for themselves but for Christ, who "died for all, so that they who live would no longer live for themselves, but for Him who died and rose again on their behalf" (2 Corinthians 5:15).

In contrast to a culture where no one accepts responsibility for anything and everyone seems to blame others for everything wrong in their life, the godly young man accepts responsibility for all his actions and seeks to live for Christ in every aspect of life by the power of the Spirit, according to the Word of God.

As godly young men demonstrate responsibility toward others, they seek to be timely and punctual, they keep their promises and commitments, they build others up (rather than tearing them down), and they always seek to give God their best. They desire, in the words of Colossians 1:10, to "walk in a manner worthy of the Lord, to please Him in all respects, bearing fruit in every good work and multiplying in the full knowledge of God." Doesn't Christ, who gave everything for us, deserve the best from us in everything? Dignified men answer this question with a bold and emphatic "Yes!"

Admiral Hyman Rickover was head of the United States Nuclear Navy for almost thirty years. His admirers and his critics held strongly opposing views about the stern and demanding admiral. For many years, every officer aboard any nuclear submarine was personally interviewed and approved by Rickover. Those who went through those interviews usually came out shaking in fear or anger and totally intimidated. Among them was former President Jimmy Carter who, as a young man, applied for service under

Rickover. This is his account of a Rickover interview in his 1975 book, *Why Not the Best?*:

I had applied for the nuclear submarine program, and Admiral Rickover was interviewing me for the job. It was the first time I met Admiral Rickover, and we sat in a large room by ourselves for more than two hours, and he let me choose any subjects I wished to discuss. Very carefully, I chose those about which I knew most at the time—current events, seamanship, music, literature, naval tactics, electronics, gunnery— and he began to ask me a series of questions of increasing difficulty. In each instance, he soon proved that I knew relatively little about each subject I had chosen. He always looked right into my eyes, and he never smiled. I was saturated with cold sweat.

Finally, he asked a question and I thought I could redeem myself. He said, "How did you stand in your class at the Naval Academy?" Since I had completed my sophomore year at Georgia Tech before entering Annapolis as a plebe, I had done very well, and I swelled my chest with pride and answered, "Sir, I stood fifty-ninth in a class of 820!" I sat back to wait for the congratulations—which never came. Instead, the question: "Did you do your best?" I started to say, "Yes, sir," but I remembered who this was and recalled several of the many times at the Academy when I could have learned more about our allies, our enemies, weapons, strategy, and so forth. I was just human. I finally gulped and said, "No, sir, I didn't always do my best." He looked at me for a long time, and then turned his chair around to end the interview. He asked one final question, which I have never been able to forget—or to answer. He said, "Why not?" I sat there for a while, shaken, and then slowly left the room.

Jesus Christ is not a harsh and intimidating master; in fact, His yoke is easy and his burden is light (Matthew 11:30). Should we not always do our best for Him?

REPRESENTATIVE

The dignified young man also represents the Lord in an appropriate and effective way. This means there is an evangelistic element to living with dignity. Notice the words before and after "dignity" in 1 Timothy 2:1–4: "I exhort that...prayers...be made for all men, for kings and all who are in authority, so that we may lead a tranquil and quiet life in all godliness and dignity. This is good and acceptable in the sight of God our Savior, who desires all men to be saved and to come to the full knowledge of the truth." In other words, God wants His children to live dignified lives so people will come to Christ. The same thought carries over to our passage in Titus 2:7–8. After telling Titus that young men should be dignified in verse 7, Paul provides a rationale for doing so in verse 8: "so that the opponent will be put to shame, having nothing bad to say about us."

> **"...God wants His children to live dignified lives so people will come to Christ."**

Dignified men are called to serve as Christ's dignitaries. Do you see the word "dignity" in "dignitaries"? Our speech, attitudes, behavior, and demeanor should enhance the reputation of the royal family to which we belong. Dignified men never forget the incredible grace and mercy they have been shown by Christ in their salvation. This salvation includes amazing blessings like the privilege of access to our Heavenly Father, the sublime joys of intimacy with Christ, and the unfading riches of our eternal inheritance.

Genuine believers are actually so wealthy that their eyes are fixed on Christ, rather than the fleeting pleasures of this world. Dignified men grow in grace and find it easier to accept the imperfections of this present world and the pains that come from living on a fallen planet. Dignified young men quickly learn the inability of material things to provide lasting satisfaction. They are quick to invest in things that are eternal because they know only those spiritual treasures will last forever. They wholeheartedly embrace the Lord's teaching in Matthew 6:33: "Seek first His kingdom and His righteousness, and all these things will be added to you."

The man of dignity is aware that he represents the King of Kings. He knows why he is here, so he lives out that purpose. He is a noble man who represents His Sovereign Lord. He is an ambassador for Christ, and in that role, his lifestyle becomes an example to the real believer. His dignified lifestyle becomes a contrast to "almost believers" (who are the same as false believers; I choose to call them "make-believers"). The young man's life of dignity will also be convicting to the unbeliever. His topics of conversation are uncomfortable to the complacent person because he is a man focused solely upon Christ and His cause. Yes, he can be creative, laugh, and enjoy life, but it never keeps him from his ultimate purpose of bringing glory to God with all he does. The dignified man lives this way in order to reach those who do not know Christ, to help awaken those in the church who have not yet turned to Christ, and to help those who do know Christ to know Him better.

We should desire to be neither flippant nor shallow, directionless nor irresponsible. Instead, we are each called to be serious, noble and committed to the purpose for which Christ left us here on earth. Dignified men wholeheartedly pursue the mission to which they have been called—to proclaim the saving message of the gospel of Jesus Christ and glorify God in all areas of their lives.

FOR PERSONAL REFLECTION & GROUP DISCUSSION:

1. What are some specific, practical examples you have seen of dignified character or behavior?

2. What are some examples of undignified behavior?

3. Why do so many people fail to take personal responsibility for their actions in our culture today, and what do you think is the solution to that problem?

4. Read 2 Corinthians 5:1–11. Why is it such a privilege to be "ambassadors" or representatives for Christ, and what motivations does Paul say should fuel us in that task?

5. Take some time to pray that God will work in your heart to give you such motivations, and that you will grow to be more dignified (especially in areas of weakness you have realized while reading this chapter).

9

LET THE MEN BE SOUND IN SPEECH
THE POWER OF WORDS

"[Be] sound in word which is irreproachable."
TITUS 2:8

Do you know the famous American short story of Philip Nolan? This fictional story demonstrates the importance of what we say and the consequences of saying the wrong thing.

Jump back in time to a small courtroom in the early 1800s. A military trial is in session and the charge of treason is brought against the defendant, a young lieutenant named Philip Nolan. He is being court-martialed for his participation in a conspiracy to set up an independent nation in the Louisiana Territory. At the end of the trial, the judge asks the lieutenant one final question: "Will you affirm your allegiance to the United States?" Brazenly, Nolan stands to his feet and declares this now famous statement: "I wish I may never hear of the United States again."

The court pronounced its verdict, and the young man got his wish: he would never hear of the United States again. He spent the rest of his life aboard a series of large ocean-going ships and was never again allowed to set foot on American soil. On top of that, the crewmen on each of those ships were forbidden to mention the United States in any way while in Nolan's presence. And anything Nolan was allowed to read was redacted to remove any references to the United States. Philip Nolan died aboard one of those ships at an old age, paying dearly for one uncontrolled statement he made as a young man.

THE IMPORTANCE OF SOUND SPEECH

Nolan's story is a reminder to all young men of the devastating consequences of even a few words. While his punishment for a misspoken word may seem bizarre because of its severity, it illustrates the type of scrutiny every Christian young man is under concerning his speech. Many people think nothing of speaking, texting, tweeting, or emailing an angry word, spreading a rumor, slandering another's character, or stating half-truths. Men casually make insinuations, utter swear words, boast about accomplishments, lie, criticize, speak contentiously, or complain constantly. They ignore the reality that, just like Philip Nolan, their speech is on trial.

When you use words in a harmful way, you forget that two of the Ten Commandments refer to the tongue and the book of Proverbs is packed with over 100 warnings against unprincipled speech. Plus the Lord Jesus Christ issued many dire warnings against the unsavory use of words. He said, "Whatever you have said in the dark will be heard in the light, and what you have whispered in the inner rooms will be proclaimed upon the housetops" (Luke 12:3).

Christians in general, and young men in particular, tend to forget that their words are powerful. The old adage "sticks and stones may break my bones, but words will never hurt me" is a lie right out of the pit of hell. Bones can break and end up healing stronger than before. But some words and some names that people are called can break a person. Words can build up or tear down, draw families, churches, and nations closer together or closer to war.

> **"...Scripture goes well beyond explaining that words are powerful— it also teaches that your speech is a thermometer of the heart."**

This is why Scripture has so much to say about our speech. The Bible addresses issues like swearing, criticizing, gossiping, lying, corrupting talk, boastfulness, and complaining, among others. But Scripture goes well beyond explaining that words are powerful—it also teaches that your speech is a thermometer of the heart. Just as a thermometer will give you a gauge of temperature, the Bible says that your speech gives everyone listening a reading of what you are really like, and what your spiritual condition is. As Jesus says in Matthew 12:34, "The mouth speaks out of that which fills the heart."

This means that if you really want to know how you are doing spiritually, or whether your heart is right before God, your gauge should not be church attendance, praying before meals, how much you give, or whether you serve in a ministry. Even though those behaviors each represent essential duties for a Christian, anyone can perform these tasks without being born again or currently obedient to Christ. Instead, to gauge your heart, you ought to be evaluating your conversations with fellow employees, your spouse, your friends and your children in light of the stark reality that Jesus Christ Himself, the Judge of mankind, is evaluating the words you speak. He also said, "Every careless word that people speak, they shall give an accounting for it in the day of judgment. For by your words you will be justified, and by your words you will be condemned" (Matthew 12:36–37). Little slips of the tongue are much more important than we often think. So young men must evaluate their speech in light of the Lord's scrutiny and judgment.

Are you able to resist the temptation to spread the latest juicy rumor or ignore the flesh when it wants to eavesdrop on tantalizing gossip? Can you avoid spewing words of harsh criticism or ungrateful complaints? Your tongue is a continual reminder of your need to follow God's Word and depend upon the Holy Spirit every moment of the day. Young men must heed the warning of James 3:9–10: "With it [the tongue] we bless our Lord and Father, and with it we curse men, who have been made in the likeness of God. From the same mouth come blessing and cursing. My brothers, these things ought not to be so." Never forget that your words are powerful—they reveal the status of your heart, and they all fall under the scrutiny of Jesus Christ.

This brings us to the last of the characteristics of the godly man mentioned in Titus 2:8: he must be "sound in word which is irreproachable, so that the opponent will be put to shame, having nothing bad to say about us." A detailed study of this verse unlocks the secrets to a controlled tongue that builds up others instead of tearing them down. Godly young men are to be known for healthy speech. From Paul's words to Titus, we learn that our daily conversations should always be true, tested, tonic, and tactical.

SOUND SPEECH IS TRUE

Godly Christian men tell the truth in what they say. The Greek term "logos," translated "word" in Titus 2:8, is most often used in the New Testament to refer to God's Word but sometimes can more generally mean the truth, or a true and trustworthy statement. It is clear that our speech is to be truthful and in no way contain any lying or deceit. You are to heed the words of Colossians 3:9: "Do not lie to one another, since you put off the old man with its evil practices." That command is a present tense verb in the Greek, so it means our whole way of life is to be marked by the absence of deceit.

"...the godly young man who is sound in his speech recognizes that a lie is any misrepresentation of the truth."

Not only that, but the godly young man who is sound in his speech recognizes that a lie is any misrepresentation of the truth. Even if our words are technically accurate, but we mislead with our tone of voice, an omission, or a gesture, we are violating God's commands.

Always speaking the truth is very difficult today because we live in a fallen world that is saturated with deception. Lying has become a way of life. There are so many forms of lying that even believers are often caught unaware of their unintentional deception. There is the open, bold-faced lie; the advertising lie (selling something and making it sound reliable when you know it's not), the "little white lie" ("tell them I'm not home"), the perspective lie (telling your spouse you saved $250 by purchasing a big-screen TV while leaving out the fact you still paid several thousand dollars), the half-truth lie (Abraham calling Sarah his "sister"), the double-meaning lie (telling someone you caught a huge fish when it was a butcher who tossed it to you), the rumor lie (passing on distorted comments about others that are unfounded or made up), the guess-the-motive lie (assigning to the actions of others an evil motive which you could never possibly know), and finally, the lie of flattery (a genuine compliment is based on truth, but all flattery is based on a lie with self-seeking motives).

I had a grandmother who flattered me. She would say, "You must be the smartest student in your school" when I had just "flunked lunch." While my face was covered with seemingly terminal acne, she was telling me that I was the most handsome junior high boy she had ever met. Her flattery didn't help but actually hurt. She was speaking obvious lies and I was wounded by her false encouragement, because I knew it had no basis of truth and made me feel worse about my shortcomings and weaknesses. I needed to hear encouraging truth, not the lies of flattery.

"...when the truth is spoken with grace and love, it ultimately will build up, heal wounds, and make others more like Christ."

Most people grow up with someone in their family who has a bent toward lying because many people avoid conflict by being untruthful. Believers too can often avoid accountability by lying. Some Christians avoid confrontation in discipleship by lying. Other times, spiritual leaders lie to hide their sin. Lying and deception have saturated our society and too often infiltrate the church. Any form of lying only pleases our enemy Satan, who is the father of lies (John 8:44).

The truth can hurt, and telling the truth can be uncomfortable in some situations. But when the truth is spoken with grace and love, it ultimately will build up, heal wounds, and make others more like Christ. At the same time, lying and deception always destroy.

"...the godly young man guards his mouth by testing his words before they are spoken."

If you want to glorify "the God of truth" (Isaiah 65:16), serve as ambassadors of the Son who is "the truth" (John 14:6), and be filled with "the Spirit of truth" (John 16:13), then you will have to be known for speaking the truth. You must hear what Solomon says in Proverbs 6:16–19: "There are six things which Yahweh hates, even seven which are an abomination to Him," and two of them are "a lying tongue" and "a false witness who breathes out lies." You need to hear the Lord's warning in Matthew 5:37: "Let your statement be, 'Yes, yes' or 'No, no'; anything beyond these is of the evil one."

You also need to consistently speak the truth in order to be like Christ. 1 Peter 2:21–22 says, "For to this you have been called, since Christ also suffered for you, leaving you an example that you should follow in His steps, who did no sin, nor was any deceit found in His mouth." Jesus always spoke the truth, the whole truth, and nothing but the truth. It was He Himself who challenged us to live a life where our yes is yes, and our no is no. Will you follow His perfect example?

SOUND SPEECH IS TESTED

A godly man will pursue living "sound in word which is irreproachable." To say that his speech is "irreproachable" refers to the fact that his conversation—at any place, or at any time—cannot be justly accused or criticized. He will always seek to reflect a heart that is currently right before Christ. In other words, the godly young man guards his mouth by testing his words before they are spoken. The most godly men in the world will regrettably admit that they have spoken words and immediately wished they could take them back. They are grieved the words came out of their mouth, but they still seek to control their tongues. So the young man who pursues Christ will seek to heed the words of Psalm 39:1, "I will keep watch over my ways that I may not sin with my tongue; I will keep watch over my mouth as with a muzzle"; Psalm 141:3, "Set a guard, O Yahweh, over my mouth; keep watch over the door of my lips"; Ephesians 5:4, "[There must be no] filthiness and foolish talk, or coarse jesting, which are not fitting, but rather giving of thanks"; and Ephesians 4:29, "Let no unwholesome word proceed from your mouth."

What those verses basically say is, "Don't let it out." In other words, even if what you are about to say may be true, God reminds you that it is not necessarily proper, best, helpful, or even allowable at that moment.

TESTING YOUR SPEECH WITH YOUR PARENTS

For a younger man who still lives at home with his parents, there are many ways to "test" your speech in that environment.

You should avoid trapping your parents in their contradictions. You know how that works: Mom says one thing, then Dad says something totally different, and you, being fairly clever, say, "Aha, I got you both!"

You might actually be right. You may have caught them in a contradiction. But who wants to live with a jerk who only listens to point out their conversational mistakes?

Understand, there are no "professional parents." This is their first and final shot at parenting, and they are not perfect. So while you can encourage your parents toward Christlikeness, primarily by your example, do not make a habit of pointing out their inconsistencies.

Also, healthy communication at home involves admitting your own mistakes. As you get older, show your parents they are still

---

"Have enough humility to admit that you do not know everything and you do not have it all together. Be vulnerable about your weaknesses, goals for growth, and even your fears."

---

needed in your life. Have enough humility to admit that you do not know everything and you do not have it all together. Be vulnerable about your weaknesses, goals for growth, and even your fears.

Finally, if you are blessed to have Christian parents and even if you don't, ask their opinion on issues. They are always asking you questions, so turn the tables on them. (You'll find that most parents are actually quite interesting.) Ask your mom about her prior dating life or ask your dad about how he courted your mother, or what he was like in college. You will not only learn some things, but it will also probably improve your relationship with them.

TESTING YOUR SPEECH WITH OTHERS

Another way to develop sound speech is to avoid repeating or encouraging gossip and slander. When you listen to or share a bad report about someone, whether intentionally or unintentionally, you are participating in unsound speech. What is a "bad report"? It is the communication of distorted facts, incomplete details, or out-of-context information, causing others to come to an incomplete or inaccurate conclusion and negatively shading their opinion of someone.

The Bible teaches that evil reports are passed on by whisperers, gossips, slanderers, and busybodies—each of whom the Bible condemns severely. As far as the Bible is concerned, there is

---

"The Bible teaches that evil reports are passed on by whisperers, gossips, slanderers, and busybodies—each of whom the Bible condemns severely."

---

little difference between a gun and a tongue. Both assassinate people, and unfortunately, some families and churches are full of verbal assassins.

How does a godly young man stop this process? How can you test your own words, as well as the words of others, to ensure you are not a gossip or a slanderer?

There are two solutions offered in Scripture. First, you need to be willing to talk less and listen more. There is a reason God has given us two ears and one mouth! As Christians, we need to become men of few words. When it is not the proper time to speak, we stay silent. Young men especially must heed what God's Word says on this subject: "The simpleminded fool multiplies words" (Ecclesiastes 10:14); and, "When there are many words, transgression is unavoidable, but he who holds back his lips has insight" (Proverbs 10:19).

If you keep talking, you will likely sin. James 1:26 says, "If anyone thinks himself to be religious while not bridling his tongue but deceiving his own heart, this man's religion is worthless." One of my favorite verses, which has kept me from much grief—though I still long to apply it more often—is Proverbs 17:28: "Even an ignorant fool, when he keeps silent, is considered wise; when he closes his lips, he is considered understanding." The meaning of that verse is simple: Just don't talk, and people will think you're smart.

Second, not only will a man with a tested tongue talk less, but he also will develop the habit of screening what he hears. When he hears information shared by someone else, he will ask questions like this: Is it true? Is it necessary? Is it kind? Is it my business? If the answer to any of those questions is no, a godly Christian man will refuse to listen to it. He will remember the words of Proverbs 17:9, which says that "he who repeats a matter separates close companions." So when you hear something you should not know, what can you do? Walk away, change the subject, or say, "Let's talk about the Lord!" Or gently confront by saying, "I have a problem with gossip, so please don't tell me anything I might pass on with your name attached to it." Or be more direct: "I don't think the Lord is pleased by this conversation."

When godly men hear unsought gossip or slander of any kind, they do not get on the phone to spread information—they go to the throne in prayer because they desire to be sound in their speech. Yes, don't go to the phone, go to the throne!

SOUND SPEECH IS TONIC

Christian men are to speak in a way that brings healing. When Paul tells Titus that his speech must be "sound," as mentioned in chapter three, the word he uses literally means "healthful." In fact, the Greek word for "sound" is used throughout the New Testament and most often means "bringing healing" or "making one whole and complete." It is the same word from which we get our English word "hygiene." This word describes that which is clean, good, and whole. In other words, our speech is to reflect what is said in Ephesians 4:29: "Let no unwholesome word proceed from your mouth, but only such a word as is good for building up what is needed, so that it will give grace to those who hear." Do your words build up and benefit your hearers? Are they tonic?

The speech of the Christian man should also reflect Colossians 4:6: "Let your words always be with grace, seasoned with salt, so that you will know how you should answer each person." Is your speech pleasant? Are you careful that what you say is expressed at an opportune time and that it is appropriate to each individual? Jesus, as in all things, is our model for tonic words. It was said of Him, "All were speaking well of Him and marveling at the gracious words which were coming forth from His lips" (Luke 4:22).

"What you speak, especially what you say about other people, is a clear indicator of what is in your heart."

What you speak, especially what you say about other people, is a clear indicator of what is in your heart. If your heart is critical, your comments will follow suit. If your heart is compassionate, your conversation will manifest love. If your heart is condemning, you will tear down others. If your heart is edifying, your comments of others will be constructive. Jesus made this pointedly clear in Matthew 15:18: "The things that proceed out of the mouth come from the heart, and those defile the man."

Men of God must continually be reminded of what Proverbs 18:21 says: "Death and life are in the power of the tongue." The words you use have incredible power to build or destroy. When it comes to our comments about other people, each one of us is either a vulture or a hummingbird. When a vulture flies over a desert, it will find a carcass to tear apart. But when a hummingbird flies over the desert, it will find a flower and seek out its nectar. When you talk about or evaluate people around you, are you looking for carcasses or flowers, put-downs or build-ups? Your tongue is either a samurai sword that brings destruction or a doctor's scalpel that brings healing.

While waiting for a flight, a friend of mine watched a severely burned girl sit down with her mother a few seats away from him. Everyone who walked by craned their necks to stare at her scarred face, and my friend could see she was uncomfortable. But an older man came and sat between my friend and the burned girl. Immediately he began to stare at her intensely. She tried to hide herself behind her mother and my friend was about to tell him to stop looking, when the older man spoke. With incredible sincerity, he said, "Excuse me miss, I am sorry for staring, but I have to tell you, you have the most beautiful blue eyes I have ever seen." What he said was true, she had luminous blue eyes. Within minutes, she was not only sitting up but smiling and laughing with the older man. What happened during that encounter was the truth of Proverbs 12:18 in action; "The tongue of the wise brings healing."

Our words can become tonic by our mastering of three simple phrases. The first is this: **"I'm sorry, please forgive me."** Unfortunately, some have learned to say "sorry" without real repentance. They say the word, but everyone around knows they do not mean it. Godly young men learn to ask for forgiveness and mean it!

The second is to say, **"That's okay, I forgive you,"** without holding grudges or keeping a list of past offenses. Godly young men have learned to forgive, forget, and refuse to bring up the past. Never keep a list. Always keep short accounts.

The third phrase to master for tonic speech is this: **"I love you."** Some of your family, parents, children, and close friends have not heard that phrase in days, weeks, months, or maybe even years. They need to be told they are loved. And, of course, if you are married, you need to routinely express your love for your wife in order to be obedient to the commands of Scripture (Ephesians 5:22–33) and not have your prayers hindered (1 Peter 3:7). Don't be like the husband who for twenty-five years of marriage failed to tell his wife he loved her. When asked why by the marriage counselor, he said, "I said it to her on our wedding day and told her if anything changed, I would let her know."

Gracious words need to be shared often. Young men need to work hard at cultivating kindness in speech. This may not seem cool, but it is Christlike. Whether it is through sincere compliments, public praise, surprise phone calls, or notes of encouragement that affirm the unique giftedness and potential of others, start using your tongue the way God intended. Your words should reflect Christ's attribute of kindness, and not the devil's destructive ways of gossip, criticism, complaints, or lies.

SOUND SPEECH IS TACTICAL

Our speech is our primary tactic to win souls for Jesus Christ. Look again at Titus 2:8. We are to be "sound in word which is irreproachable." Why? Let's explore the rest of that verse for the answer: "So that the opponent will be put to shame, having nothing bad to say about us."

"If a godly young man was put on trial for his words, there should be no legitimate accusation against him."

Why should your speech be true, tested, and tonic? So it can be your tactic to share Christ. Paul wants Titus to make sure his speech is above reproach—without blame—so that the false teacher or secular leader will have nothing bad to say. There will be no evidence for a court to convict or find fault. If a godly young man was put on trial for his words, there should be no legitimate accusation against him.

The Scribes and Pharisees plotted against Christ, to catch Him in something He might say. Some things never change.

Throughout your life there will be unbelievers at work, school, or even home, who will try to discredit you, using your words against you. So consider your speech carefully—your words are the primary method by which you proclaim Christ.

This is why complaining is so devastating to the cause of Christ. Do you recall Philippians 2:14–15? "Do all things without grumbling or disputing." This means you should never express dissatisfaction or skeptical questioning of God or His Word, nor should you be sinfully critical of other people. Your speech is your reputation. Your words are your testimony. Your talk is to be radically different from the world's. If Christians are complainers, then how is that different from the unsaved? If you grumble and criticize, what do you have to offer the world that they do not already have? Nothing!

Paul continues in the next verse: "So that you will be blameless and innocent, children of God without blemish in the midst of a crooked and perverse generation, among whom you shine as lights in the world" (Philippians 2:15).

Complaining will never contribute anything to being a light to the world. If you complain, you are acting no different than those without Christ. So never forget why you are here. There is one thing, and only one thing, that you can do for God here on earth that you will not be able to do in Heaven. And that is to use your tongue to share Christ with those who do not know Him. When you get to heaven, that opportunity, privilege, and responsibility will be gone forever.

If you look at the verse before Paul's command about grumbling and disputing in Philippians 2, you will see that those sins are a direct insult to the Sovereign God who orders all the events you are complaining about. Philippians 2:13 says, "It is God who is at work in you, both to will and to work for His good pleasure." God is sovereign, so when you complain, you are insulting the One who is in control of every detail of your life.

You who serve the King of the universe, the God of abundant

grace, the Savior who loves and forgives and empowers us, should have the most positive, encouraging, and delightful things to say. People around you will want Christ if you begin to practice sound speech. Or, at least they will have "nothing bad to say about us," as Titus 2:8 says. So share the truth; share the gospel; tell people about Christ. And do not give them any reason to reject Him.

People are listening to what you say. Will they find your speech to be true, tested, tonic, and an effective tactic for sharing the gospel?

FOR PERSONAL REFLECTION & GROUP DISCUSSION:

1. What are some examples of unwise words that have caused severely negative consequences for the person who said them?

2. Jesus said, "The mouth speaks out of that which fills the heart" (Matthew 12:34). What are some sinful heart attitudes that contribute to unsound speech, and what are some biblical cures for them?

3. What are some times that the words of others have been "tonic" or healing for you?

4. Pick a psalm of praise from the book of Psalms that you can memorize and pray to the Lord whenever you are tempted to grumble and complain.

5. Take some time to pray for your speech and the heart attitudes at the root of it.

10

LET THE MEN BE PREPARED
THE HOPE FOR THE FUTURE

*"The honor of young men is their strength, and
the majesty of old men is their gray hair."*
PROVERBS 20:29

Every major sport has a short list of elite athletes, past and present, that have competed at the highest level. Names like Michael Jordan, LeBron James, Wayne Gretsky, Mike Trout, Clayton Kershaw, Richard Petty, Jerry Rice, and Tom Brady are recognizable to many of us because of their consistent contributions to their respective sports. Each of these so-called "superstars" cultivated daily disciplined habits that prepared them for the competition. Their ability to consistently bring their "A game" started long before the game clock. And their ongoing commitment to these habits is what allowed them to enjoy long-term success.

I find it interesting that when Paul wrote to Titus about Christian men, he didn't just speak about all of them in general but addressed the older men and then the younger men as separate groups. And he addressed the older men first. Perhaps one of the reasons for this is that he wanted the younger men to have something to shoot for—to have a "big picture" or "long-term view" in mind of what they could and should become in the future. That kind of goal-oriented thinking helps young men work hard in the present and for a long time into the future, staying the course through thick and thin and not giving up through the ebb and flow of success and failure during the course of their lives.

Titus 1:5–9 presents an exciting goal for the future of young men when it describes the calling and qualifications for leading men (elders) in Christ's church, and Titus 2:2 adds to that by saying, "Older men are to be temperate, dignified, sensible, sound in faith, in love, in perseverance." This is truly something great for young men to shoot for—to one day become the kind of older men who can change the world by their godly example and set a course of ministry that others can imitate.

What can you do now in your younger life that will prepare you for a future of effectiveness in serving your Savior and Lord Jesus Christ? This book has provided many answers to that question already, but let us summarize much of what we've learned. I want to leave you with an understanding of five commitments that set godly young men apart and make them ready for great tasks for God's glory.

A COMMITMENT TO GOD'S DESIGN

First, you must be committed to pursuing your role as a man according to God's Word. That's the primary purpose of this book —to aid you in the pursuit of God's design for men in headship, priorities, and Christlike character qualities. And to understand and live out your God-given roles in singleness, marriage, family, and in the church.

God's plan is for men to lead in their homes and in the church. Sadly, because many young Christian men have not developed convictions, they are not anchored to Biblical wisdom. They don't know what to look for in a spouse, how to function in marriage, how to lead others in the church, or how to impact the world. But the man who understands God's design for men and lives out that blueprint will be greatly used by God. He will be an ambassador for Christ in his God-given roles as husband, father, employee, and church leader.

"The pursuit of fulfilling God's design for a man while single is what prepares a future husband for marriage..."

It is crucial that young men, even prior to marriage, begin to build biblical convictions about the role of a man. They do this first by learning what the Word of God says about men and then by following the example of godly older men who model God's design in every aspect of their lives. A church full of men who are pursuing the Word of God is the perfect environment for young men to mature into manhood. The pursuit of fulfilling God's design for a man while single is what prepares a future husband for marriage, even assisting him in the choice of a lifelong mate.

In a sermon on 1 John 2:13, where the Apostle mentions "young men," the great preacher Charles Spurgeon described God's design in his unique way:

> *In speaking to young men in Christ, I am speaking to*
> *a numerous body of Christians among ourselves, who*

make up a very efficient part of the army of Christ in this region....

They are not yet fathers because they are not yet so established, confirmed, and settled as the fathers are, who know what they believe, and know it with a certainty of full assurance which nothing can shake. They have not yet had the experience of fathers, and consequently have not all their prudence and foresight: they are richer in zeal than in judgment. They have not yet acquired the nursing faculty so precious in the church as the product of growth, experience, maturity, and affection; they are going on to that, and in a short time they will have reached it, but as yet they have other work to do more suitable to their vigour....

These young men are born to fight; they are the militia of the church, they have to contend for her faith, and to extend the Redeemer's kingdom. They should do so, for they are strong. This is their lot, and the Lord help them to fulfill their calling. These must for years to come be our active spirits: they are our strength and our hope. The fathers must soon go off the stage: their maturity in grace shows that they are ready for glory, and it is not God's way to keep his shocks of corn in the field when once they are fully ripe for the garner— perfect men shall be gathered up with the perfect, and shall enter into their proper sphere. The fathers, therefore, must soon be gone; and when they are gone, to whom are we to look for a succession but to these young men? We hope to have them for many years with us, valiant for the truth, steadfast in the faith, ripening in spirit, and growingly made meet to take their seats among the glorified saints above. Judge ye, dear brethren, whether ye are fairly to be ranked among the young men. (The Metropolitan Tabernacle Pulpit, Volume 29)

A COMMITMENT TO GROWING MATURITY

The passage that Spurgeon preached from is very helpful in encouraging young men to have the big picture and long-term view mentioned earlier. Here is that whole section of Scripture: "I am writing to you, little children, because your sins have been forgiven you for His name's sake. I am writing to you, fathers, because you have known Him who has been from the beginning. I am writing to you, young men, because you have overcome the evil one. I have written to you, children, because you have known the Father. I have written to you, fathers, because you have known Him who has been from the beginning. I have written to you, young men, because you are strong, and the word of God abides in you, and you have overcome the evil one" (1 John 2:12–14).

What this means, among other things, is that young men should strive to grow to maturity. Men who love God should desire to know God more intimately. Young men who desire to be impactful for Christ should grow to be more like Christ.

The good news is that the Lord promises He will complete that process if you are truly His child. Philippians 1:6 says, "For I am confident of this very thing, that He who began a good work in you will perfect it until the day of Christ Jesus." The negative side to this promise is found in Hebrews 12:14: "Pursue peace with all men, and the sanctification without which no one will see the Lord." If there is no sanctification in your life, no growth, no progress in becoming like Christ, that raises the question of whether you are a genuine born-again Christian.

Progressive sanctification is absolutely essential for the assurance of salvation and becoming all that God wants you to be. But what steps do you have to take as a young man to grow into that older, respectable man of God? Spiritual growth will not happen by

"Spiritual growth will not happen by osmosis—you will have to put forth a lot of effort, empowered by the Holy Spirit and motivated by the gospel of grace."

osmosis—you will have to put forth a lot of effort, empowered by the Holy Spirit and motivated by the gospel of grace.

Most believers already know that growing in spiritual maturity requires a life of dependence upon the Holy Spirit as they seek to follow only the Word of God day by day. And this growth will definitely involve your commitment to "the means of grace" or "the spiritual disciplines." These include the study, meditation, memorization, and sharing of God's Word. Additional actions include prayer, fellowship, involvement in a local church, service in ministry, enduring trials, proclaiming the gospel, discipleship, and fleeing the flesh while pursuing Christlike qualities. These are all essential for growth and young men would be wise to make them priorities in their weekly schedule.

It is also important to emphasize that the primary motivation for practicing the means of grace is the gospel of grace. There is no greater incentive for pursuing spiritual maturity than remembering what Christ has done for us and being grateful for it. We see this motivational priority reflected in the structure of both Romans and Ephesians. Before Paul says in Romans 12:1–2 that we should present ourselves as a living sacrifice to God and be transformed by the renewing of our minds, he spends eleven chapters (Romans 1–11) telling us about the gospel and various truths that help us to understand it better. And before he speaks about the importance of pursuing spiritual maturity in Ephesians 4:13–16, Paul teaches us about the gospel of grace for three chapters prior to that. Clearly, the great Apostle believed that what Christ has done for us is foundational to what we should do for Him.

Be careful not to get this motivational order backwards. If we think that we have to "measure up" in order to receive the benefits of Christ, we will be prone to despair in failure or take pride in our success. But realizing that "we love, because He first loved us" (1 John 4:19) will keep us from despair—even though we will

> ## "If we think that we have to 'measure up' in order to receive the benefits of Christ, we will be prone to despair in failure or take pride in our success."

fail in many ways. No believer will ever perfectly live up to the truths drawn from God's Word discussed in this book. But every young Christian man can know that God has chosen him by His grace to become like His Son, and that process of sanctification will continue all the way until heaven (Philippians 1:6, Romans 8:28–30). Being motivated by His saving grace before pursuing the means of sanctifying grace will also keep you from pride when you succeed because you will remember "it is God who is at work in you, both to will and to work for His good pleasure" (Philippians 2:13). From start to finish, God deserves all the glory.

A COMMITMENT TO DISCIPLESHIP

The Great Commission found in Matthew 28:19–20 is a command for us today. In that passage, Jesus says, "Go therefore and make disciples of all the nations, baptizing them in the name of the Father and the Son and the Holy Spirit, teaching them to keep all that I commanded you; and behold, I am with you always, even to the end of the age."

"Discipleship is best defined as intentional relationships for the purpose of coming to Christ and becoming like Christ."

Discipleship is best defined as intentional relationships for the purpose of coming to Christ and becoming like Christ. In the Great Commission Jesus describes the main verb of "make disciples" by three participles—going, baptizing, and teaching. All the verbs are plural, which means that discipleship can be done in groups, not just in one-on-one relationships. But regardless of how many people are involved, discipleship is always expressed in intentional, purposeful relationships.

The main verb **make disciples** of Matthew 28:19-20 is explained by the three participles in the two verses. The participle **going** describes discipleship as a relational commitment to evangelizing as you walk through life as a believer. The participle **baptizing** describes discipleship as relationally identifying with Christ and immersion into His Body, the church. And the participle **teaching** them to obey describes discipleship as the relational process of helping one another to learn and obey God's Word in every aspect of life.

The ultimate goal of discipleship is not just to have people come to Christ, but also to immerse themselves in a church body while identifying with Christ alone as their Lord, and to become followers of Christ who live every aspect of their lives under the authority of God's Word, including making disciples themselves.

Discipleship is the Lord's plan to transform this world. The Great Commission was the briefing before the battle. Discipleship is essential to the individual Christian and the mission of every local church—yet so few churches are committed to practicing it. Sadly, the discipleship process is often relegated to a small percentage of a church family who are serious about Christ. But Christ's intention was for every believer and every church corporately to be whole-heartedly committed to the process of discipleship. As Christians, we must understand that the Lord Jesus designed our relationships with each other to be a powerful means of grace, to make us more like Christ and to impact the world with the gospel.

> **"...Christ's intention was for every believer and every church corporately to be whole-heartedly committed to the process of discipleship."**

In a one-on-one meeting with just two men or in a meeting with a small group of men, discipleship should involve prayer and discussion about every element of the Christian life. Marriage, family, work, recreation, relationships, ministry, thought life, and battles with sins like lust, greed, and pride are all fair game. You need to apply the Scripture to those areas until more and more of your life is lived according to the Word and not the world, by the Spirit and not the flesh, and by principles rather than preferences.

Discipleship should be one of the highest priorities in the life of a young man. You must be discipled by a godly man or—even better—a group of godly men, in the context of a church that is filled with those who embrace discipleship, until you learn how to lead a group and disciple others. Imagine what it would be like to be discipled by a group of men who are all pursuing Christ in a church of people who are all pursuing Christ together! How great would it be if the vast majority of relationships in your life were with born-again believers who want to be like Christ? It would be an incredible blessing that would lead to amazing growth, fruitful ministry and prepare you to make a profound impact on the world.

Discipleship is crucial, essential, vital, and not optional. Why am I making such a big deal about this? In addition to the fact that it was Jesus' last command before he ascended to heaven, here is one more reason: discipleship is parenting and parenting is discipleship. The word "parenting" does not occur in the Bible, but "making disciples" does. The process of parenting is the process of discipleship. The young single or married man who has been discipled and has learned to make disciples is best prepared for raising children. A young godly man who can disciple others is a man who can parent his children.

"Cultivate intentional relationships for the purpose of the gospel and growth in Christ."

If you want to know whether a woman you are courting can raise children biblically, you simply have to determine if she has discipled other women. Has she been fruitful in her discipleship efforts? And if you are wondering about how you can prepare now to become the father you hope to be someday, then learn now how to make disciples. Cultivate intentional relationships for the purpose of the gospel and growth in Christ.

A COMMITMENT TO CHURCH

The Bible commands all believers to faithfully attend church. Hebrews 10:24–25 is very direct: "And let us consider how to stimulate one another to love and good deeds, not forsaking our own assembling together, as is the habit of some, but encouraging one another, and all the more as you see the day drawing near."

The church by nature is a gathering of believers. You cannot have an assembly of Christians unless you actually assemble. And notice that even in this command to faithfully gather there is more intended than mere attendance. We are to love one another and stimulate one another to good works. The church is more than a business, it is a body. It is more than gathering, it's ministering your gifts. It is more than spectating, it is participating.

As each member of the church functions according to God's Word, we all become more like Christ. Ephesians 4:16 says, "From [Christ] the whole body, being joined and held together by what every joint supplies, according to the properly measured working of each individual part, causes the growth of the body for the building up of itself in love." In that verse, Paul makes it clear that your growth in Christ is inseparably linked to your participation in a healthy local church. Instead of being independent, young men are to be dependent upon a local church family.

OUR OBLIGATION TO BE INTERCONNECTED

In addition to Hebrews 10:24–25, more than forty other commands appear in Scripture for believers to exercise "one anothers" (as stated in chapter three). To expand on the prior list—have the same mind with one another, do not judge one another, be devoted to one another, serve one another, be subject to one another, build up one another, do not speak against one another, live in peace with one another, pray for one another, and many more.

There are also commands for you to minister to others

in the church using your unique gifts, which were given to you by the Holy Spirit at the point of salvation. Each genuine believer has a God-given ability for service in the body of Christ. 1 Peter 4:10–11 says, "As each one has received a gift, employ it in serving one another as good stewards of the manifold grace of God—whoever speaks, as one speaking the oracles of God; whoever serves as one serving by the strength which God supplies; so that in all things God may be glorified through Jesus Christ, to whom belongs the glory and might forever and ever. Amen."

Remember, Jesus said in Matthew 23:11 and Luke 22:26 that "the greatest among you shall be your servant." No one can be considered a godly man or a godly woman who is not a servant. Service to the body of Christ is essential for all believers and is the pathway for a young Christian man to mature in Christ.

Through faithful ministry over time, a young man learns the unique way God has made him and the specific plan God has for him. The apostle Paul makes a dramatic statement in Ephesians 2:10: "For we are His workmanship, created in Christ Jesus for good works, which God prepared beforehand so that we would walk in them." God announces that he has already pre-selected good works for each Christian to live out in his or her life. Just like Jeremiah was pre-chosen to be a prophet and Paul was pre-chosen to be an apostle, every believer is pre-chosen to uniquely live out some good works on this planet before heaven.

> **"...God has a purpose for you, but you will only discover what His purpose is when you are faithful in ministry over time in the context of a local church."**

Acts 13:36 says, "David, after he had served the purpose of God in his own generation, fell asleep and was laid among his fathers and saw corruption." David fulfilled his purpose during his lifetime. God had a purpose for him and God has a purpose for you, but you will only discover what His purpose is when you are faithful in ministry over time in the context of a local church.

OUR NEED FOR ONE ANOTHER IN THE CHURCH

The growth of a godly young man is linked to his inter-connectedness to a local church. No one man has all spiritual gifts, so becoming more like Christ and enjoying the fullness of Christ will happen when you are immersed in a healthy local church.

The "one another" commands in the New Testament are given to members of local churches and are meant to be lived out in those local churches. Together we are to submit to biblical leadership under the headship of Christ, give faithfully and sacrificially, participate in communion and church discipline, preserve unity, protect each other from error, learn sound doctrine from biblical preaching, proclaim the gospel, pursue the process of discipleship, and much more.

Young men are to follow the example of older men in a local church. Paul's exhortation in 1 Corinthians 11:1, "Be imitators of me, just as I also am of Christ," was written to the members of a church he founded. Peter also is speaking to church members in 1 Peter 5:5 when he says, "You younger men, likewise, be subject to your elders. And all of you, clothe yourselves with humility toward one another, for God is opposed to the proud, but gives grace to the humble." Older godly men are to train up younger men in the context of the church and younger men are to be humble enough to seek wisdom and follow their example.

Relational intimacy and ministry interconnection within a local church are not an option for the young man who desires

---

> "The church is God's plan for this age.
> There is no other plan, and a young
> man needs to embrace that conviction
> early and carry that conviction with
> him throughout his entire life."

---

to be godly and impactful for Christ. The church is God's plan for this age. There is no other plan, and a young man needs to embrace that conviction early and carry that conviction with him throughout his entire life. A godly man will share his passion for Christ's church with his wife and pass it on to his children and grandchildren. Regardless of the church's weaknesses and shortcomings, young men must become fans of the church - the church is the bride of Christ and the apple of His eye. Even in a culture where independence and individuality reign supreme, the godly young man will pursue inter-dependence and community in a local church. It is God's will and young men desperately need it.

A COMMITMENT TO THE GOSPEL

For a young man to have the hope of one day becoming an exemplary older man, he must also commit himself to proclaiming the gospel to lost people and seek to live worthy of it.

The gospels prove to all that our Lord has a compassionate heart for those who are lost and a desire for us to proclaim the gospel to them. Matthew 9:36–38 says, "Seeing the crowds, He felt compassion for them, because they were distressed and downcast like sheep without a shepherd. Then He said to His disciples, 'The harvest is plentiful, but the workers are few.

Therefore pray earnestly to the Lord of the harvest to send out workers into His harvest.'"

The Great Commission commands believers to go out into the world and proclaim the gospel. The theme verse of Acts, at the very beginning of the book, tells us why God has left us here on this planet: "You will receive power when the Holy Spirit has come upon you; and you shall be My witnesses both in Jerusalem, and in all Judea and Samaria, and even to the end of the earth" (Acts 1:8).

The Epistles continue this emphasis by affirming that all believers are to be praying for wisdom in how to share with the lost, both with our conduct and with our communication. Colossians 4:5–6 says, "Walk in wisdom toward outsiders, redeeming the time. Let your words always be with grace, seasoned with salt, so that you will know how you should answer each person."

Proclaiming the gospel is one of the main reasons God left us here. In a discussion with my mentor John MacArthur, I came up with a way to help believers think through the priority of evangelism. I like to ask them, "What is your purpose in life?" They will say, "To glorify God." Then I ask, "Can you glorify God better in heaven or on earth?" The answer is heaven, since you will be perfect in heaven.

"If that is your purpose," I say, "and you can glorify God better in heaven than on earth, then why doesn't God take you immediately to heaven once you get saved - why does God leave you here on earth?" The answer I give is, "The reason the Lord leaves you here on earth is to do here what you cannot do in heaven."

Next I ask, "What can you do on earth that you cannot do in heaven?" If they are not staring at me blankly, they will answer saying either, "Share the gospel with the lost," or, "have children!"

For the believer, these two reasons are actually one and the same. Why do Christian parents have children? So that the children may come to Christ and follow Christ. The reason why God left us on earth is to glorify Him here by doing what we can't do in heaven - which is to proclaim the gospel and model the gospel with the lost as well as our own children. The Gospel is why our God leaves us here!

We are here on planet earth to share the gospel. The gospel is primarily a message, not merely a lifestyle. Paul does challenge believers to live worthy of the gospel in Philippians 1:27, but the rest of the New Testament continually declares that the gospel is good news; the gospel is a message to be told. The gospel is the good news of how God saves sinners. It is a message about how those who are condemned by God because of their sin can be made right with God. God saves sinners, so now believers are left on earth to proclaim the message that Jesus Christ, God's Son who lived a perfect life, offered Himself as our substitute, died for our sin on the cross, rose from the dead, and ascended into heaven.

Because of God's great love and mercy, the Father sent the Son to live a perfectly obedient life, to take the punishment you deserved on the cross and to rise again from the dead so you could have a new life in Him. As Paul says in 1 Corinthians 15:3–4, "For I delivered to you as of first importance what I also received, that Christ died for our sins according to the Scriptures, and that He was buried, and that He was raised on the third day according to the Scriptures."

It is faith in the death and resurrection of the only perfect One that provides the only way of salvation. You exchange your sin for

---

> ## "All believers are to know, love, and obey Christ. But our mission while on earth is to proclaim the message of the gospel."

His righteousness; you surrender your life and embrace His life; you exchange all that you are for all that He is; you embrace Christ by turning from your sin in repentance and depending on His life and death by faith. Only then can you be saved.

All believers are to know, love, and obey Christ. But our mission while on earth is to proclaim the message of the gospel. Only those young godly men who learn to share the gospel and adorn it by their lives will be used greatly of God, fulfilling their purpose and functioning the way God designed. The Great Commission says "Go," the Greek participle literally meaning "as you are going." As you go through life in this world, you are to be sharing the gospel with all who are lost.

HOPE FOR THE FUTURE

Commitment to these five foundations: God's Design, Growing in Maturity, Discipleship, The Church, and The Gospel are crucial for young men to grow into godly older men who will become influential leaders in the church and in the world. These commitments set certain young men apart to be used in great ways by our gracious King. It is my prayer, not merely to let the men be men, but also for each man to make a great impact in this life for God's glory.

My hope is that each man reading this book will see the Lord accomplish in his life what Paul describes in Ephesians 3:20–21: "Now to Him who is able to do far more abundantly beyond all that we ask or understand, according to the power that works within us, to Him be the glory in the church and in Christ Jesus to all generations forever and ever. Amen."

FOR PERSONAL REFLECTION & GROUP DISCUSSION:

1. What are your hopes and goals for the future? Do they include becoming a godly older man who will be an influential leader in the church and the world? Why or why not?

2. Where do you think you are on the "spiritual maturity scale" in 1 John 2:12–14, and why? Ask at least two others who know you well where they think you are and why.

3. How would you answer someone who says, "I go to church on Sundays—isn't that enough?" Use at least two Scripture passages in your answer.

4. Colossians 2:6 says, "As you received Christ Jesus the Lord, so walk in him." Why do you think the gospel is not only necessary for non-Christians to come to Christ, but also for Christians to walk in Christ?

5. Take some time to pray, thanking God for His grace to you (mentioning some specific promises and provisions), making the commitments discussed in this chapter, and asking Him to enable you to keep them by the power of the Holy Spirit.

God's Plan of Salvation

Everyone is destined to die, but life does not end with death. The Bible says that after death there will be a judgment where each person will give an account of his life to God (Hebrews 9:27). When God created Adam and Eve in His own image in the garden of Eden, He gave them an abundant life, and the freedom to choose between good and evil. They chose to disobey God and go their own way. As a consequence, death was introduced into the human race, not only physical death, but also spiritual death. For this reason, all human beings are separated from God.

Unfortunately, man's fallen nature and his on-going choices to sin, results in men living in continual disobedience to God: *for all have sinned and fall short of the glory of God (Romans 3:23)*. This is humanity's problem: because of sin everyone is separated from God (Isaiah 59:2).

People have tried to overcome this separation in many ways: by doing good, by practicing religion or creating their own ideas of salvation, or by attempting to live a good, moral and fair life. However, none of these things is enough to cross the barrier of separation between God and humanity, because God is holy and human beings are sinful. Regardless of how good you think you are, each and every human being has lied, stolen, been angry, lusted, hated, hurt others, resisted God and defied His perfect character.

This spiritual separation has become the condition of mankind, and because of this they are condemned: *He who believes in Him is not judged; he who does not believe has been judged already, because he has not believed in the name of the only begotten Son of God (John 3:18).*

God's Love and Plan

Jesus Christ said:

> *For God so loved the world, that He gave His only begotten Son, that whoever believes in Him shall not perish, but have eternal life (John 3:16).*
> *I came that they may have life, and have it abundantly (John 10:10).*
> *He who believes in the Son has eternal life; but he who does not obey the Son will not see life, but the wrath of God abides on him (John 3:36).*
> *I am the way, and the truth, and the life. No one comes to the Father but through Me (John 14:6).*

God's holiness makes it impossible for Him to relate to sinful humanity, and His justice demands that every sinner be judged and condemned to an eternal separation from God. Because of this, all people have become the enemy of God. Although God has every right to condemn every single person, because of His love He provided a solution through His Son, Jesus Christ. God knew people could not save themselves, so God determined to save sinners. God sent His Son, Jesus Christ, 100% God and 100% man, to bear the sins of His children on the cross. Jesus' death was the only acceptable sacrifice for sin: *And there is salvation in no one else, for there is no other name under heaven that has been given among men by which we must be saved (Acts 4:12).*

When Jesus died on the cross, He paid the penalty for the sins of His children – the penalty which was death – and thereby established a bridge between God and people. Anyone who puts their trust in Christ can be saved. Because of this sacrifice, every person who is born again can have true fellowship with God now and forever.

Jesus Christ Is Alive Today

After Jesus Christ died on the cross at Calvary, where He received the punishment that we deserved, the Bible says that He was buried in a tomb. But He did not remain there: Christ rose from the dead! For all those who believe in Jesus Christ, His resurrection is a guarantee that they will also be resurrected to eternal life in the presence of God forever. This is very good news! *Christ died for our sins...was buried, and...He was raised on the third day according to the Scriptures (1 Corinthians 15:3-4).*

How to Receive God's Love and Plan

In His mercy, God has determined that salvation is free. To receive it, agree with and believe these four things:

1. Acknowledge your deadly problem. You are a sinner by nature, and you have chosen to sin repeatedly violating God's law and missing the mark of God's perfect character. Because you have sinned, you have missed God's perfect plan for you and you are separated now from God.

2. Repent, by turning from your hated sins, and put your faith in Christ by being completely dependent upon Christ, trusting in His Work on the cross to provide you with salvation, forgiveness of sins, abundant life now and eternal life forever.

3. Publicly acknowledge that Jesus Christ is God, who died, taking your place on the cross for your sins, then because He had no sin of His own, rose from the dead, ascended into heaven and is the only one who can make you right with God.

4. Then, from a new heart that wants to obey (Romans 6:17), get to know Christ by learning His Word, love Christ by treasuring His Word and follow Christ by obeying His Word.

The Bible says:

> *...that if you confess with your mouth Jesus as Lord, and believe in your heart that God raised Him from the dead, you will be saved (Romans 10:9).*
> *...for "Whoever calls on the name of the Lord will be saved"(Romans 10:13).*

A Prayer to Receive Jesus Christ

Cry out to Christ Jesus and beg Him to awaken your heart that is dead and your mind that is blind, and ask Him to give you a NEW HEART that can express Faith in Him and Repent from sin. Admit that you cannot save yourself. That no one but Christ can deliver you from sin. Acknowledge that Christ is God who alone can make you right with God now and forever because of His death on the cross and His resurrection from the dead.

When He saves you, you will look the same on the outside but you will not be the same on the inside. You will have a willingness to do whatever Christ wants (Luke 14). You will want to obey His Word (Romans 6:17), gather with His people and worship Him by offering your entire life to Him (Romans 12:2), follow Him in every aspect of life in order to know Christ more intimately as your first love (Revelation 2:7).

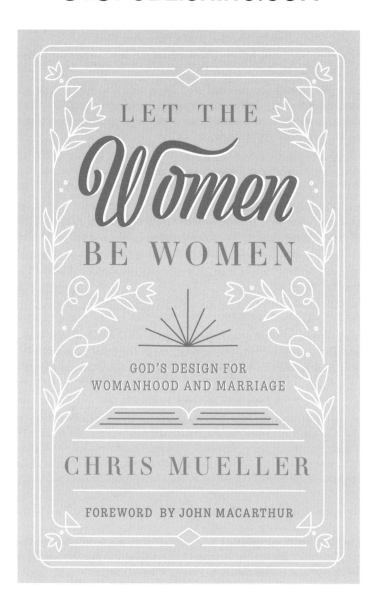

LET THE

Women

BE WOMEN

GOD'S DESIGN FOR
WOMANHOOD AND MARRIAGE

CHRIS MUELLER

FOREWORD BY JOHN MACARTHUR

LEGACY
STANDARD
BIBLE

read.LSBible.org

CONNECT WITH US!

THREE SIXTEEN PUBLISHING

Sign up for announcements about new Bibles, books and more.

316PUBLISHING.COM